MW00651120

EXPERIENCING CHICK COREA

The Listener's Companion
Gregg Akkerman, Series Editor

Titles in **The Listener's Companion** provide readers with a deeper understanding of key musical genres and the work of major artists and composers. Aimed at nonspecialists, each volume explains in clear and accessible language how to *listen* to works from particular artists, composers, and genres. Looking at both the context in which the music first appeared and has since been heard, authors explore with readers the environments in which key musical works were written and performed.

Experiencing the Beatles: A Listener's Companion, by Brooke Halpin
Experiencing Beethoven: A Listener's Companion, by Geoffrey Block
Experiencing Bessie Smith: A Listener's Companion, by John Clark
Experiencing Billy Joel: A Listener's Companion, by Thomas MacFarlane
Experiencing Broadway Music: A Listener's Companion, by Kathryn Sherrell
Experiencing Carl Maria von Weber: A Listener's Companion, by Joseph E. Morgan
Experiencing Chick Corea: A Listener's Companion, by Monika Herzig
Experiencing Chopin: A Listener's Companion, by Christine Gengaro
Experiencing David Bowie: A Listener's Companion, by Ian Chapman
Experiencing Film Music: A Listener's Companion, by Kenneth LaFave
Experiencing Jazz: A Listener's Companion, by Michael Stephans
Experiencing Led Zeppelin: A Listener's Companion, by Gregg Akkerman
Experiencing Leonard Bernstein: A Listener's Companion, by Kenneth LaFave
Experiencing Mozart: A Listener's Companion, by David Schroeder
Experiencing Peter Gabriel: A Listener's Companion, by Durrell Bowman
Experiencing the Rolling Stones: A Listener's Companion, by David Malvinni
Experiencing Rush: A Listener's Companion, by Durrell Bowman
Experiencing Schumann: A Listener's Companion, by Donald Sanders
Experiencing Stravinsky: A Listener's Companion, by Robin Maconie
Experiencing Tchaikovsky: A Listener's Companion, by David Schroeder
Experiencing Verdi: A Listener's Companion, by Donald Sanders
Experiencing the Violin Concerto: A Listener's Companion, by Franco Sciannameo

EXPERIENCING CHICK COREA

A Listener's Companion

Monika Herzig

ROWMAN & LITTLEFIELD
Lanham • Boulder • New York • London

Published by Rowman & Littlefield
A wholly owned subsidiary of The Rowman & Littlefield Publishing Group, Inc.
4501 Forbes Boulevard, Suite 200, Lanham, Maryland 20706
www.rowman.com

Unit A, Whitacre Mews, 26-34 Stannary Street, London SE11 4AB

British Library Cataloguing in Publication Information Available

Library of Congress Cataloging-in-Publication Data

Names: Herzig, Monika, 1964- author.
Title: Experiencing Chick Corea : a listener's companion / Monika Herzig.
Description: Lanham : Rowman & Littlefield, [2017] | Series: The listener's companion | Includes bibliographical references and index.
Identifiers: LCCN 2017018138 (print) | LCCN 2017018714 (ebook) | ISBN 9781442244696 (electronic) | ISBN 9781442244689 (cloth : alk. paper)
Subjects: LCSH: Corea, Chick—Criticism and interpretation. | Jazz—History and criticism.
Classification: LCC ML417.C79 (ebook) | LCC ML417.C79 H47 2017 (print) | DDC 786.2/165092—dc23 LC record available at https://lccn.loc.gov/2017018138

∞ ™ The paper used in this publication meets the minimum requirements of American National Standard for Information Sciences Permanence of Paper for Printed Library Materials, ANSI/NISO Z39.48-1992.

Printed in the United States of America

To my family and mentors who supported me throughout this journey of becoming a jazz musician, educator, and author, most of all to my husband and musical companion of three decades, Peter Kienle, and my children Zackary and Jasmin.

In memory of master educator David Baker, I hope this book will inspire readers to explore jazz as a creative art form just as David Baker inspired me.

CONTENTS

Series Editor's Foreword ix
Preface xi
Introduction: Putting the Jazz in the Piano xiii
Timeline xxi

1 *Now He Sings, Now He Sobs*— What Was? 1
2 *Bitches Brew* and *In A Silent Way* 13
3 Circle—An Avant-Garde Excursion 23
4 Return to Forever— The Acoustic Years 31
5 Return to Forever—Electric 41
6 Playing with Friends 57
7 Acoustic Variations 67
8 Back to Electric 77
9 So Many Things To Do 91

Coda: The Corea Legacy 105
Notes 109
Selected Discography 123
Selected Reading 129
Index 133
About the Author 139

SERIES EDITOR'S FOREWORD

The goal of the Listener's Companion series is to give readers a deeper understanding of pivotal musical genres and the creative work of their iconic composers and performers. This is accomplished in an inclusive manner that does not necessitate extensive music training or elitist shoulder rubbing. Authors of the series place the reader in specific listening experiences in which the music is examined in its historical context with regard to both compositional and societal parameters. By positioning the reader in the real or supposed environment of the music's creation, the author provides for a deeper enjoyment and appreciation of the art form. Series authors, often drawing on their own expertise as both performers and scholars, deliver to readers a broad understanding of major musical genres and the achievements of artists within those genres as lived listening experiences.

The music of Chick Corea has fascinated jazz fans since the late 1960s and his career and inventiveness are far from over. Introduced to a vast audience through Miles Davis's *Bitches Brew* albums, it was apparent that Corea was a transformational keyboardist. Bud Powell had modernized the approach to playing chords in the jazz idiom, and Bill Evans beautifully refined these ideas. But both of these artists had recognizable influences from their peers or musicians who preceded them. With Corea, the lineage is murky. Like guitarist Jimi Hendrix or vocalist Janis Joplin, Corea seemed to be dropped from the heavens with fully formed ideas not found gestating in any other creative minds. And yet, when other creatives heard Corea for the first time there was a collective recognition: "Of course that is where jazz keyboard needs to go." It all seemed so obvious *after* hearing Corea. But beforehand, only Herbie Hancock was on the cusp of a similar paradigm shift.

Corea's importance to the development of contemporary jazz makes him a most worthy topic for the Listener's Companion series, and Dr. Monika Herzig has done a phenomenal job presenting a guided pathway through his music. The fact that her subject is still alive and producing new music makes the task of reviewing Corea's output challenging, but Herzig shows the greatest of skill in presenting the content in the context of time and place. I have seldom worked with an author more dedicated to "getting it right" and honoring the fans of Corea's music who would not tolerate a diluted approach to the music they love. As Herzig walks you through Corea's career as a sideman or leader, performer or composer, and role model or jazz celebrity, you will benefit from an author whose intimate knowledge of the material, relevant personal interviews, and conversational writing style delivers the keenest of insight as the music reaches your ears for the first or hundredth time.

Gregg Akkerman

PREFACE

One of the first jazz pieces that I learned on the piano was Chick Corea's "Spain." I fell in love with the lighthearted yet sophisticated music that was quite challenging but made people dance, laugh, and get inspired—emotionally and intellectually. Once I discovered that we shared our day of birth, June 12, I was hooked—the music spoke to me in such a special way. I learned as many tunes as possible, transcribed and learned solos, and finally got to see my first live concert in 1987—the Acoustic Trio with Dave Weckl and John Patitucci in Tübingen, Germany. I was actually working on my undergraduate thesis at the time where I compared the piano styles of Art Tatum, Thelonious Monk, and Chick Corea. The concert was inspiring and creative and after the audience had left, Chick was sitting at the piano onstage just noodling away. With the little English I knew at the time, I went up and told him about my thesis project and asked him questions about piano stylings. He was more than happy to demonstrate examples and explain his piano lineage. It was a fascinating lesson and I thanked him as we left—but, alas, my little Walkman had failed to record, and the conversation and lesson was only recorded in my memory.

I completed my thesis a few months later and received a scholarship for an exchange program at the University of Alabama. This was our opportunity to pursue our dreams of becoming jazz musicians, so my boyfriend—now husband of more than twenty-five years—and I sold all our belongings and bought one-way tickets. It was the best decision we made: we got to tour the world; open for acts such as Sting, Yes, and

Santana; and record many albums with wonderful musicians including Bob Berg—and I also completed a doctorate at Indiana University where I currently teach in the arts management program.

Over the years, I had several more opportunities to experience Chick Corea in live settings—the Elektric Band in Indianapolis in 1992, Chick Corea with Eddie Gomez and Jack DeJohnette at the 2006 International Association of Jazz Educators (IAJE) conference in Atlanta, the duo with Bela Fleck at the 2007 Indy Jazz Fest, with Bobby McFerrin and Jack DeJohnette at Butler University's Clowes Hall in 2008, at the Tokyo Blue Note with Lenny White and Stanley Clark in 2009, the Hot House tour with Gary Burton at the Palladium in Carmel, Indiana, in 2014 where I was able to provide a preconcert talk, and finally, the last concert of eighty for the seventy-fifth birthday celebrations at the Blue Note in New York with John McLaughlin, Bela Fleck, Victor Wooten, and Lenny White in 2016! Every time it became clear that this is an artist who is true to his musical vision, never making any compromises, and always performing at the top of his capacities.

In addition, I collected as many recordings and songbooks as possible, always drawing inspiration from my birthday partner. I never had the opportunity for a personal conversation again until the 2016 Blue Note concert thanks to my amazing manager Suzi Reynolds. It was a very special moment when I shared with Chick about my opportunity to put this book together, and I hope that the information and listening guides will inspire many readers as much as Chick Corea inspired my musical career.

Much appreciation goes to everyone who was willing to provide an interview and additional information and the team and editors at Rowman & Littlefield for including this volume in the Listener's Companion series. Of course, many thanks to my husband, Peter Kienle, and children, Zackary and Jasmin Herzig, for allowing me the time to write and research. And of course, my gratitude goes to Chick Corea himself for all the wonderful music and inspiration over the years.

INTRODUCTION

Putting the Jazz in the Piano

The piano is a unique instrument: it is a percussion instrument with strings that can play melody, harmony, and bass all at the same time. It can serve as an accompanying instrument and it can act as lead instrument. In fact, the piano is the most popular instrument in the world, both as a concert instrument as well as the primary instrument in private homes. The two oldest preserved pianos, built by Bartolomeo Cristofori (1655–1731), date back to 1720 and 1726 and are housed at the Metropolitan Museum of Art in New York City and in a museum in Leipzig, Germany, respectively. Cristofori invented the current hammer action in 1709, a combination of the dulcimer strike of the strings initiated by the keyboard touch, which made it possible for the instrument to play loud and soft, hence the name *pianoforte*. As is often the case with new inventions, the pianoforte was initially rejected by the masters who had been performing and writing for the harpsichord and clavichord. But even Johann Sebastian Bach finally acknowledged the superior quality and sound of the new instrument when he tested craftsman Gottfried Silbermann's model at the court of Frederick the Great in 1747. Bach's sons, Philipp Emanuel and Christian, as well as Wolfgang Amadeus Mozart and Muzio Clementi, were among the first composers who wrote music showcasing the full range of capabilities of this new instrument and helped its successful introduction to the rest of the world.

The piano became an essential piece of furniture in every American classroom, and between 1870 and 1930 the second most expensive budget item in every house purchase besides the house itself was the piano. The image of mother seated at the keyboard with the children gathered around her next to the father in pinstriped shirt and suspenders became the symbol of the American dream. Throughout the nineteenth century, the piano-making industry grew rapidly, and division of labor through a specialized supply industry made it possible to produce larger quantities at lower cost. This was a significant step, as traditionally all instruments had been constructed as a whole. Also important to consider is that more than six thousand sections and small parts, springs, and strips have to be put together for one single piano mechanism. The manufacturing process became especially efficient in the United States, and American piano manufacturers soon covered half of the world's supply until the Great Depression marked the downturn of the booming piano industry as most households were no longer able to afford a piano as well as piano lessons.

Because of its size, the piano had not gained importance as a band instrument. Early brass bands performed mostly at picnics, parades, and funerals and thus relied mostly on portable instruments, with guitars and banjos covering the harmonic accompaniments. In addition, performance and teaching practices at that time included very little training in improvisational techniques. Improvisation was common practice for musicians during the baroque and classical period when performers often concluded their concerts with an improvisation on a theme provided by the audience. But a new performance ethic evolved, focusing on the interpretation of the score rather than showcasing the performer's improvisatory skills and virtuosity, during the romantic period. Austrian pianist Artur Schnabel (1882–1951) was one of the proponents of a purist approach for taking the spotlight away from the performer and focusing on the inner thoughts of the composer. Thus improvisational practices were eliminated from classical performance etiquette and consequently from musical training. As a result, most serious pianists were not interested in adapting the jazz style to the piano, and instruction in improvisation is still not a common feature in classical piano training.

As the hot rhythms of jazz with the call-and-response techniques from field hollers and the expressive qualities of the blues spread across the United States during the early decades of the twentieth century, ragtime became the musical adaptation of the new style for the piano. Early ragtime composers, such as Scott Joplin, used classical dance forms while attempting to translate the sound of popular brass bands to the piano. The interplay of two hands was ideal for capturing the accompaniment of the banjo and the rhythms of the dances. Thus, ragtime pieces were condensed versions of brass band arrangements with the left hand covering the trombone, guitar, and tuba parts and the right hand simulating the soaring clarinet embellishments and the cornet leads. Ragtime became the earliest documented form of jazz piano and the most popular music style in America from 1900 to 1918. Initially, ragtime was through-composed music and since keyboard training in the European tradition was a required skill for middle-class white women, they were the main customers who bought sheet music of those colorful rags in droves. In addition, piano rolls for the player pianos featured many ragtime pieces and became the record players of the day.

However, there are limits to what a piano can do with respect to any effort to performing in a "hot" style. Hitting a key, which in turn strikes a string, doesn't allow for bending and sliding between notes or changing sonorities as can be done on guitars and wind instruments. As early jazz bands developed "hot" techniques for playing instruments in new expressive ways, pianists experimented with strategies to capture the sound and excitement of a brass band. New Orleans pianist Jelly Roll Morton (1885–1941) boasted that he invented jazz in 1902 by successfully meshing classical ragtime with the ethnic styles of New Orleans, a claim highly disputed by his critics. Nevertheless, his recordings demonstrate his inventive style and his compositions became some of the first pieces clearly identified with the jazz idiom. Morton was a highly paid performer in Storyville, the red-light district of the New Orleans French Quarter. After Storyville was shut down, Morton traveled to the West Coast and eventually settled in Chicago where he formed the Red Hot Peppers. He successfully translated his piano style and New Orleans roots into the compositions and arrangements recorded with the Red Hot Peppers as exemplified in classics such as "Grandpa's Spells" and "Black Bottom Stomp."

Simultaneously, pianist Eubie Blake (1883–1983) honed his skills in the "sporting houses" of Baltimore and eventually New York. Initially a self-taught ragtime pianist and composer, he became known for his celebrated technique and ability to perform easily in all twelve keys. Some of his early gems composed with lyricist Noble Sissle include "I'm Just Wild about Harry," "Memories of You," and "Lucky to Be Me." He eventually earned a degree from New York University and was rediscovered during the 1969 Newport Jazz Festival, followed by frequent recordings until he reached the ripe age of nearly one hundred.

The liberation of the piano style by the likes of Morton and Blake away from the ragtime compositions to stomps and struts that incorporated the energy and improvisational techniques of early jazz laid the foundation for the development of the "stride" piano technique. While the left hand "strides" in steady motion from a bass note to a chord in the middle register usually at a fast pace, the right hand incorporates improvisational techniques and bluesy phrases by striking grace notes while expanding the harmonic language of ragtime with fuller harmonies and chromatic passages. After 1910, all-night gatherings called rent parties became popular strategies for raising funds to pay the host's rent in urban centers with pianists entertaining all night. Competition between pianists and the need to perform at breakneck tempos for extended periods spurred the need for better technique and improvisational skills. Great examples of the stride techniques and level of virtuosity are Charles Luckeyeth "Luckey" Roberts (1895–1968), Willie "The Lion" Smith (1897–1973), Thomas "Fats" Waller (1903–1943), and James P. Johnson (1891–1955), often referred to as the father of stride piano. In fact, James P. Johnson's trademark composition, "Carolina Shout," was the first jazz piano piece that pianist Bud Powell learned growing up in Harlem. Chick Corea refers to Bud Powell as one of his idols during his teenage years in terms of fluency and compositional styles,[1] hence establishing a direct lineage to the stride piano masters.

The trio of Smith, Waller, and Johnson ruled the "cutting" contests at Harlem rent parties. It was customary for pianists to outplay each other at such parties and solicit acknowledgment from the audience on the winner by speed, virtuosity, and inventiveness. James P. Johnson was Fats Waller's tutor who became known for improvising more complex, sophisticated, and symmetrical right-hand melodies than any of his predecessors. But eventually all competitors found their master in Art Tatum (1909–1956), a legally blind pianist hailing from Toledo, Ohio.

His virtuosity was unparalleled and his level of swing and harmonic inventiveness pushed all known boundaries. Pianist and educator Billy Taylor suspected that one of the reasons Tatum acquired such superior skills was that he initially learned by imitating piano rolls, which often had additional notes added after the fact.[2] Nevertheless, Tatum figured out how to create the same effect with just two hands. In 1933, he made his way to New York as an accompanist for vocalist Adelaide Hall, and Smith, Waller, and Johnson challenged him to a cutting contest. In his biography of Art Tatum, Lester Johnson shares this anecdote by Waller's son, Maurice Waller:

> Art played the main theme of Vincent Youmans' big hit, "Tea for Two," and introduced his inventive harmonies, slightly altering the melodic line. Good, but not very impressive. Then it happened. Tatum's left hand worked a strong, regular beat while his right hand played dazzling arpeggios in chords loaded with flatted fifths and ninths. Both his hands then raced toward each other in skips and runs that seemed impossible to master. Then they crossed each other. Tatum played the main theme again and soared to an exciting climax.
>
> The entourage was stunned; lulled by Fats [Waller's] preliminary assessment, they hadn't expected anything near Tatum's level of virtuosity. But gamely they tried to meet the challenge. James P. followed Tatum with "Carolina Shout," playing, Maurice Waller writes, "As if his hands were possessed by a demon. But it wasn't good enough." Waller then presented his showpiece, "A Handful of Keys," but Tatum still had the edge. Then Art came up once more and roared through "Tiger Rag." James P. tried one more time, with his version of Chopin's "Revolutionary Etude." "Dad told me he never heard Jimmy play so remarkably," Maurice Waller concludes, "but the performance fell short. Tatum was the undisputed king." Later on, James P. would admit, "When Tatum played 'Tea for Two' that night, I guess that was the first time I ever heard it really *played*."[3]

The marriage of stride piano and blues techniques reached its popular height from 1935 to 1939 in the form of boogie-woogie's repetitive bass figures based on the blues form and clever right-hand blues riffs often performed at breakneck speed. This short-lived style flourished mainly in the midwestern cities of Chicago and Kansas City and the rhythmic feeling was quite reminiscent of a freight train clacking down the track. Legendary jazz producer John Hammond was instrumental in discovering and recording some of the boogie-woogie masters including two Chicago taxicab drivers, Meade Lux Lewis and Albert Ammons (groundskeeper for the Chicago White Sox Jimmy Yancey), and Kansas City pianist Pete Johnson. He brought them to New York where they became major concert attractions, often performing together with blues singer Big Joe Turner. But the repeated bass riffs and blues licks did not offer enough variations to its fans and flexibility for the musicians, and by 1940 the boogie-woogie craze faded.

The piano had finally found equal status as a jazz instrument. Initially a solo instrument or in a supportive role in the swing-era big bands, it now became an effective member of any ensemble and small combo. This evolutionary step marks the beginning of modern jazz piano. Early examples of the developing interplay with the other combo members by transferring some of the stride chords of the left hand to the bassist and incorporating modern harmonies and melodies from the horn players are the Nat King Cole Trio and Teddy Wilson's style with the Benny Goodman Quartet.

During the 1940s, jazz in general transitioned from music for dancing to music for listening. Several factors contributed to this evolution of a new style called bebop, or bop. The military draft had thinned out the ranks of the big bands, and the city of New York established a 20 percent cabaret tax on clubs that had dancing and floor shows. In addition, jazz musicians had been experimenting in after-hours jam sessions with extended harmonic and melodic vocabulary beyond the common major and minor scales. The added tax expense motivated club owners to host small ensembles and support the modern sounds more suited for listening.

One of the legendary jam session spots was Minton's Playhouse in Harlem. When former bandleader Teddy Hill took over management of the club in 1940, he established Monday night jam sessions and invited musicians to come in after their regular engagements and interact free from the constraints of commercial entertainment jobs. Two members of the paid house band, drummer Kenny Clarke and pianist Thelonious Monk, became the backbone for a host of young players ready to develop a more complex, intimate, and expressive musical style. This willingness of pushing the boundaries and exploring new territory has always been the philosophical essence of jazz since the early days of meshing musical traditions with new ways of playing. Initially succeeding as entertainers, an underprivileged class was able to make a triumphant statement. On the other hand, the boundaries of pure entertainment now caused friction with the quest for exploration and new means of expression. Hence, the table was set for new directions and the late night jam sessions provided the opportunity to develop a new musical language called bebop. Similar to ragtime, bebop became a way to absorb and transform other musical genres. American popular songs became the harmonic vehicles for a highly individualized treatment of melody through systematic alteration, substitution, and extension of those chord structures. One of the piano innovators, Mary Lou Williams, recalls:

> He [pianist Thelonious Monk] was one of the original modernists all right, playing pretty much the same harmonies then that he's playing now. Only in those days we called it "Zombie music" and reserved it mostly for musicians after hours. Why "Zombie music"? Because the screwy chords reminded us of music from *Frankenstein* or any horror film. I was one of the first with these frozen sounds, and after a night's jamming would sit and play weird harmonies (just chord progressions) with Dick Wilson, a very advanced tenor player.[4]

Instrumental among the frequent jam session participants were Kansas City saxophonist Charlie Parker and trumpeter Dizzy Gillespie. Initially the two met during a jam session when Dizzy Gillespie came through Kansas City with Cab Calloway's Orchestra. They connected through similar ideas and their quest for new sounds, and when they reunited just a few months later in New York, their enthusiasm was infectious. In addition, their high level of artistry and musicianship set the bar for their fellow musicians. Unfortunately, much of the early development of bop is not documented on recordings due to a recording ban by the Musician's Union from 1942 to 1944 who believed that recordings killed job opportunities for live musicians.

The music that emerged during the after-hours jamming was a significant departure from its origins in New Orleans. Focus had shifted from entertainment to art, from ensemble to individual expression, from dance rhythms to explosive intensity, and the seeds for jazz as an artistic expression were planted. Inspired by the sophisticated horn melodies of Dizzy Gillespie and Charlie Parker, pianists developed similar melodic phrasings as part of their improvisational repertoire. Pianist Clyde Hart, who accompanied Parker and Gillespie in 1944, was one of the first to free the left hand from the tradition of striding in order to focus on the right-hand melodies. As a result, the strict time-keeping function of the left hand on every beat rooted in the ragtime style was replaced by simple accents often using only two- or three-chord tones and complementing the shape and accents of the right-hand melodies.

Bud Powell (1924–1966) became the bop pianist par excellence, combining all the modern stylistic elements that pianists had been exploring during the 1930s and '40s. Equipped with excellent technique from studying European classics, he developed a fluid hornlike melodic style in his right hand punctuated by sophisticated harmonic accents in the left hand. His improvisational style was flawless and displayed all the bop elements described earlier and his influence on the pianists who followed him was profound. After Powell started frequenting the Minton's jam sessions at age fifteen, Thelonious Monk took the talented but troubled teenager under his wing. Unfortunately, Powell fought a battle with depression and schizophrenia that drove him into mental institutions multiple times, and he spent his later years in Europe hoping to escape the pressures from home. Some of his lasting compositions include "Bouncing with Bud," "Dance of the Infidels," "Wail," "Tempus Fugue-It," "Celia," and "Hallucinations." Chick Corea confirms Powell's influence on his music:

> Bud Powell has been an ongoing musical flame throughout my life. He was very influential as a teacher through his recordings, all through my growing up with music. Everything about his playing and the way he approached his music had an attraction for me. There was always an incredible depth, but also an incredible straightforwardness and honesty and down-home quality to the way he would play. No matter what physical condition he was in or all the so-called ups and downs that is given so much spread. I could always just hear Bud. There he was, doing this thing that is just Bud, and that's the thing, of course, which people love him for.[5]

TIMELINE

1901 Grandfather Antonio Corea immigrates to the U.S. from Albi, Italy.

1941 On June 12, Armando Anthony "Chick" Corea is born in Chelsea, MA, son of Armando John and Anna Corea.

1945 Anna Corea decides to purchase an upright piano at a funeral, which has to be lifted through the third-floor window with a crane.

1952 The family purchases a home in Everett, MA, and Chick Corea gets his own room to practice piano and talks his dad into getting him a drum set.

1954 Chick Corea joins the lounge band the Four Sounds and plays his first gig. He also helps out with Phil Barboza's Latin group with conga player Bill Fitch, who teaches him different styles and eventually introduces him to Don Alias.

1959 Corea moves to New York and starts jamming in the loft scene with Tony Williams, Don Alias, Gene Perla, and others.

1960 Corea has his first major engagement with Mongo Santamaria.

1962 The first recording to document his love for Latin rhythms with Mongo Santamaria titled *Go Mongo* is released on Riverside Records.

1964 On July 30, Corea gets to record with Blue Mitchell's group *The Thing to Do* for Blue Note Records, including his own "Chick's Tune."

1966 On recommendation of bassist Steve Swallow, Stan Getz invites Chick Corea to join his group and he performs on piano again after an eighteen-month hiatus focusing on the drums.

1966 Corea is a member of Sarah Vaughn's and Herbie Mann's groups until 1968.

1967 His first recording as a leader for the Vortex/Atlantic label, *Tones for Joan's Bones* featuring Steve Swallow, Joe Farrell, Joe Chambers, and Woody Shaw, is released.

1968 The trio recording *Now He Sings, Now He Sobs* on the Solid State label with Miroslav Vitous and Roy Haynes becomes one of the most influential jazz trio recordings in history.

1968 Miles Davis replaces Herbie Hancock with Chick Corea and records additional tracks on the release *Filles de Kilimanjaro.*

1969 Miles Davis's electric period begins with the release of *In a Silent Way* featuring Chick Corea on keyboards, produced by Teo Macero.

1970 *Bitches Brew*, Miles Davis's second electric release on Columbia Records with Chick Corea on keyboards, becomes arguably the most revolutionary album in jazz history.

1970 The avant-garde group Circle forms with Chick Corea, Dave Holland, Barry Altschul, and later Anthony Braxton and releases a series of recordings on Blue Note and ECM before Corea breaks up the group in 1971.

1971 Chick Corea discovers Scientology and changes musical directions initially with the ECM recordings *Piano Improvisations Volume 1 & 2.*

1971 In November, Corea's new group Return to Forever, featuring Stanley Clarke, Joe Farrell, Airto Moreira, and Flora Purim, debuts at the Village Vanguard for an audience of eighteen.

1972 The self-titled debut album of *Return to Forever* features Corea's classic "La Fiesta," and the 1973 follow-up recording *Light as a Feather* features his hit "Spain."

1973 The ECM release *Crystal Silence* marks the beginning of a lifelong duet partnership between vibist Gary Burton and Chick Corea.

1973 Polydor releases *Hymn of the Seventh Galaxy*, featuring the new, electric version of Return to Forever with Chick Corea, Lenny White, Stanley Clarke, and Bill Connors.

1974 Nineteen-year-old guitar wiz Al Di Meola replaces Bill Connors for the "classic quartet" version of Return to Forever, which released *Where Have I Known You Before*, *No Mystery* (first Grammy Award 1975), and *Romantic Warrior* (Return to Forever's best-selling album).

1976 Corea forms a new incarnation of Return to Forever with various brass and string sections and Gayle Moran Corea on vocals and keyboard, producing the Grammy Award–winning *The Leprechaun*, *My Spanish Heart*, *Musicmagic*, and a four-LP box set.

1977 Chick Corea places twelve times in eleven different categories in the annual *DownBeat* magazine Readers Poll.

1978 An almost "impossibly active year" results in three studio albums and two live releases including *The Mad Hatter*, *Friends*, and *Secret Agent*, and *An Evening with Herbie Hancock and Chick Corea* and *Return to Forever—Live*.

1981 The recording of *Three Quartets*, an attempt to transfer the concept of chamber music to a jazz combo, marks the beginning of a five-year period focused on acoustic music. Most notable projects during this period are *Lyric Suite for Sextet*, a collaboration with Gary Burton; a reunion with Miroslav Vitous and Roy Haynes on *Trio Music*; and the flamenco-inspired recording *Touchstone*; as well as duets with Steve Kujala (*Again and Again*) and Friedrich Gulda (*The Meeting*). Corea also publishes and records his collection of twenty piano miniatures, *Children's Songs*, in 1984.

1982 Drummer Lenny White invites soul star Chaka Khan for a jazz recording project on Elektra Records. Chick Corea arranges several Great American Songbook standards, and, due to Khan's limited availability for touring, Nancy Wilson joins the Griffith Park Collection for a second recording.

1982 On June 27, Friedrich Gulda invites Chick Corea to perform a duet at the Munich Piano Festival. Corea gets inspired by Gulda's quotation of a piece by W. A. Mozart, leading to an ongoing love affair with Mozart's music. He performs and records Mozart's Double Piano Concerto with Friedrich Gulda, Keith Jarrett, and Makoto Ozone, as well as writes numerous compositions inspired by the study of Mozart's music, such as the *Septet for Winds, Strings, and Piano*, and collaborates with Bobby McFerrin on the 1996 release *The Mozart Sessions*.

1985 Inspired by new technologies and the development of the Musical Instrument Digital Interface (MIDI), Corea forms a new project incorporating electronic sounds into new compositions. The Chick Corea Elektric Band, featuring initially Dave Weckl, John Patitucci, and Scott Henderson, and later Frank Gambale and Eric Marienthal, releases the self-titled debut on GRP Records followed by six years of extensive touring and recording. The group reunited for the 2004 release *To The Stars* and for a 2016 reunion tour.

1989 Together with John Patitucci and Dave Weckl, Corea forms the Akoustic Band—an acoustic side project of the Elektric Band that allows the trio to showcase their virtuosity and straight-ahead jazz explorations.

1992 Corea launches his own label, Stretch Records, under the GRP umbrella as a platform to facilitate artistic vision and stretch musical boundaries. One of the first releases is John Patitucci's *Heart of the Bass*. The label becomes Corea's personal recording outlet in 1996 when GRP consolidates with Universal Music Group. At the dawn of the digital age, Corea leaves the label under the administration of Concord Music Group.

1993 Corea forms the Elektric Band II and releases *Paint the World* and his last release for GRP Records, *Time Warp*, in 1995.

1997 Corea's first release for his own Stretch label, *Remembering Bud Powell*, features a cast of young lions including saxophonists Joshua Redman and Kenny Garrett, trumpeter Wallace Roney, bassist Christian McBride, and legendary drummer Roy Haynes.

1998 Inspired by the artistry of young Israeli bassist Avishai Cohen and his group's recording for Corea's Stretch label, he invites Avishai with his group for a weeklong residency at New York's Blue Note club. Under the name Origin, the group releases a live set from the residency and a 1999 studio recording titled *Change*. The group receives Best Album, Best Acoustic Group, and for Corea Artist of the Year Honors in the 1999 *DownBeat* Critics Awards.

2000 Corea records his first symphonic work with Origin and the London Symphony Orchestra, *Corea.concerto*, and receives another Grammy Award. That same year he also releases a double CD set of solo piano arrangements and originals.

2001 Repeating the concept of the Chick Corea Akoustic Band, he forms the New Trio with the rhythm section of the group Origin, Avishai Cohen and Jeff Ballard, and releases *Past, Present & Futures.*

2002 On the suggestion of Blue Note manager Sal Haries, Chick Corea starts a tradition of celebrating landmark birthdays with extended residencies featuring many of his ensembles and collaborators at the Blue Note club in New York. In celebration of his sixtieth birthday, he features nine ensembles during a three-week residency with the subsequent release of the Grammy-winning *Rendezvous in New York*.

2004 The reunited Elektric Band tours and releases *To The Stars*, and with different personnel Corea follows up with *The Ultimate Adventure*. Both recordings feature tone poems based on characters from L. Ron Hubbard's sci-fi novels.

2005 Various collaborations in Europe produce *Live in Molde* with the Trondheim Jazz Orchestra and *Touchstone*, a live compilation from a tour with flamenco musicians Paco DeLucia, Carles Benavent, Jorge Pardo, and Rubem Dantas as well as drummer Tommy Brechtlein and special guest Gayle Moran Corea.

2005 Throughout the next decade, starting with the April 3, 2005, live recording of the Super Trio (with Christian McBride and Steve Gadd) at the One World Theatre, Corea starts an intense exploration of the intimate piano trio settings with the six-box set *Five Trios*, the 2012 tribute to Bill Evans *Further Explorations*, and the 2014 formation of Trilogy with Christian McBride and Brian Blade.

2006 Chick Corea receives the Jazz Masters Award from the National Endowment of the Arts, the highest honor for any jazz artist.

2006 Corea continues various duet partnerships with the genre-crossing *Enchantment* featuring banjo virtuoso Bela Fleck, duo piano encounters with Hiromi (*Duet*, 2007), Stefano Bollani (*Orvieto*, 2011), celebrating his longtime partnership with vibraphonist Gary Burton with *The New Crystal Silence* (2008) and the 2012 Grammy-winning *Hot House*, and the double live album *Two* with Bela Fleck in 2015.

2008 The highly anticipated reunion tour of Return to Forever with Al Di Meola, Stanley Clarke, and Lenny White is documented in the release *Returns* and a live DVD from the Montreux Jazz Festival. Another extensive reunion tour with special guests in 2012 is documented on the double CD *The Mothership Returns* as well as a full-length documentary. Corea's hometown names a street in his honor.

2009 With fellow Miles Davis alum and fusion pioneer John McLaughlin, Corea forms the Five Peace Band, realizing their forty-year-old dream of having a band together.

2010 *DownBeat* magazine honors Chick Corea as Jazz Artist of the Year, Electric Keyboardist of the Year, and inducts him in the Hall of Fame—a grand slam.

2011 The acoustic trio version of Return to Forever with Chick Corea, Stanley Clarke, and Lenny White gets the spotlight throughout nearly fifty live concerts and the release of *Forever*. Nearly forty years of collaboration were rewarded with a three-Grammy sweep at the 2011 Awards for Best Latin Instrumental Album, Best Improvised Solo, and Best Jazz Instrumental Album.

2012 Corea performs and records his six-movement suite for jazz quintet and chamber orchestra with members of the Harlem Quartet and Imani Winds—*The Continents.*

2013 The cover for the release *The Vigil* with a new large ensemble features Corea as an armed warrior riding into the sunset according to his mantra "Flood the market with music—refine the art of living—defy the existing norm—keep on creating."

2014 A whimsical booklet titled *Creativity and Doodling* featuring Corea's art sketches accompanies the release of *Solo Piano—Portraits* with music by Bela Bartok and Alexander Scriabin as well as improvised portraits of audience members.

2015 The year concludes with honors by the Jazz Journalist Association naming Corea Keyboard Player of the Year and *DownBeat* magazine honoring him as Artist of the Year.

2016 Celebrating his seventy-fifth birthday, Corea hosts an unprecedented eighty-concert celebration at New York's Blue Note featuring all the facets of his career. The series includes reunions of Return to Forever, the Elektric Band, Origin, the Three Quartets Band, as well as concerts focusing on flamenco music, electronic experimentations, the music of Miles Davis, and various duets.

2017 Concord Music releases a four-disc set, *Chick Corea: The Musician*, that chronicles a month of live sets at New York's Blue Note jazz club and features a full-length documentary Blue-Ray disc.

I

NOW HE SINGS, NOW HE SOBS— WHAT WAS?

Music and jazz musicians were part of daily life at the Corea household in Chelsea, Massachusetts, with trumpeter Armando John Corea leading his band, Armando and His Orchestra, during the 1930s and '40s. His son, Armando Anthony "Chick" Corea, born on June 12, 1941, recalls many after-gig gatherings in the Corea kitchen with mother Anna whipping up a tasty frittata while his dad's fellow musicians piled into the small three-room apartment. Learning music was almost like acquiring language for little Armando Anthony, and seeing all the musicians laughing and chatting in their tuxes in the kitchen every weekend groomed his desire to be involved in music. Grandfather Antonio Corea immigrated to the United States around 1901 from Albi, Italy, a little town in Catanzaro in the south of Italy. Several of the thirteen children got involved in music, but formal music education was not an option in such a large family. Nevertheless, Corea's father Antonio became proficient on drums, piano, trumpet, and bass and was the main arranger for his Dixieland group that also included brother Frankie on trumpet. But during the after-hours gatherings in the Corea kitchen, the guys would listen to the modern bebop musicians, such as Dizzy Gillespie, Charlie Parker, and Miles Davis. Corea recalls:

> My dad had a stack of 78-rpm vinyl, and that's what he played all the time. That's what I grew up listening to. I still remember the smell of the vinyl and the yellow Dial label with Bird and Diz and Miles and the Billy Eckstine Big Band.[1]

An aunt kept pinching his cheeks calling him "cheeky, cheeky"—and the nickname stuck: Armando Anthony became "Chick" Corea. When he was four years old, his mother, Anna, decided to purchase an upright piano at a funeral. Since the staircase was too small, the piano was lifted through the third-floor window with a crane. Hence, the large piece of furniture entered with lots of commotion and excitement and little Corea was hooked. His father provided assistance in finding the notes on the piano and on paper and learning some tunes, and at age nine Corea started formal lessons with concert pianist and family friend Salvatore Sullo. Sullo introduced Corea to the classical piano repertoire and the music of Bach, Chopin, and Beethoven.

The little kid who could play was quite popular among the family's musician friends and encouraged to entertain at any occasion. Becoming anything else than a musician never entered young Corea's mind. At age eleven, mother Anna had saved enough money from her work at a candy factory to purchase a home for the family in Everett, Massachusetts, right next to Chelsea. Corea finally got his own room downstairs to practice piano and managed to talk his dad also into getting him a drum set, his second love.

A lounge band called the Four Sounds invited a teenage Corea to be their pianist—his first professional break as a mere eighth grader. The group played a variety of lounges in the area, but during practice time at home Corea's focus was on transcribing Horace Silver Quintet records. The simplicity yet effectiveness of Horace Silver's compositions attracted Corea right away and he learned the group's repertoire by slowing down the turntable and transcribing little bits at a time—not only the compositions but also Horace Silver's solos and Blue Mitchell's trumpet solos. He studied the melodic, harmonic, and rhythmic elements of the tunes and eventually, during the last year of high school, formed a trio that focused on Horace Silver repertoire. Trumpeter and educator Herb Pomeroy found out about the trio and invited them to open for his popular big band at a Boston club called the Stable, quite an honor for the young musicians. And just a few years later, the opportunity arose to be the pianist in Horace's band under Blue Mitchell's leadership—how fortuitous. Corea credits Horace as an inspiration not only through his compositions, but his philosophy of communicating with the audience:

> I practically transcribed that whole record. But I loved everything that Horace did. Horace's . . . Not just his composition. His whole communicative way of . . . It was kind of to me like pop music, Horace's music. It was delicious and palatable and grooving and made me happy.[2]

Besides his engagements with the Four Sounds, occasional gigs with a Latin group under the leadership of trumpeter Phil Barboza also proved influential on his career. Playing for dances and observing how the infectious Latin rhythms became the life of a party and made people happy laid the seeds for Corea's lifelong affinity for Latin music styles. The conga player in the group, Bill Fitch, introduced Corea to recordings and common rhythmic conventions. He became a good friend and after Corea moved to New York in 1959, he connected him with fellow conga player Don Alias and some jamming opportunities with young drummer Tony Williams. Corea's love for Latin rhythms and his connection with Bill Fitch were instrumental in getting his first major New York engagement with Mongo Santamaria in 1960. Of course, a weeklong engagement with Cab Calloway's band during Corea's junior year in Boston proved an attractive addition to the young musician's resume while building his network in the New York music community.

Besides playing with Mongo's band over the next two years, Corea frequented jam sessions and immersed himself into the New York scene. Together with saxophonist Pete Yellin he formed a rehearsal band where they added salsa and mambo beats to their favorite Charlie Parker songs. His knowledge and love for Latin rhythms is first documented on the 1962 Riverside recording *Go Mongo*, with Corea holding down piano duties for the Mongo Santamaria band. An interesting twist of fate is that Mongo's break into the mass market with his version of Herbie Hancock's "Watermelon Man" came after Corea decided to leave the group. Herbie got the call to sub for Corea with Mongo's band in a Cuban nightclub with three people in the audience. The band started to get experimental and Herbie showed them his new blues tune called "Watermelon Man." Everyone started jamming along and the tune became a staple of Mongo's repertoire. Legendary Riverside producer Orrin Keepnews encouraged a recording of the tune and it became a Top 10 pop hit in 1963 and launched Santamaria's success with his winning mix of jazz, R&B, and Latin music.

In the meantime, trumpeter Blue Mitchell asked Corea to join his band, which was the Horace Silver Quintet without Horace. The opportunity was a dream come true given that Corea had spent his last year of high school playing Horace Silver's music and copying Silver's and Mitchell's solos. At the end of this chapter, find a guided listening experience of "Chick's Tune" as recorded on Blue Mitchell's Blue Note recording *The Thing to Do*, Corea's first original composition on record documenting his excitement of working with his heroes.[3]

The realities of providing for a family with two young children and living in New York City proved quite a challenge throughout these early years. Corea took any paying engagements that kept him from getting a cab license—playing in lounges, synagogues, and casuals with wedding bands. The quality of pianos available for such casual engagements was often questionable and Corea got so discouraged playing bad pianos that he decided to perform exclusively as a drummer for an eighteen-month period. This proved to be a fertile period for composing and developing his piano style with rehearsal bands, though. Bassist Gene Perla recalls the jamming scene with percussionists Bill Fitch and Don Alias, who were most influential in developing Corea's proficiency in Latin American rhythms:

> And, so Don had met Bill and they were really good friends and Chick came along, because of some gigs they were doing. So, they gave him a bunch of records and he went home and a few days later he came back and ka koon ka koon ka koon, he had it all together.[4]

A call from saxophonist Stan Getz in 1966 to join his group as a pianist finally provided the opportunity for sufficient income and playing on a tuned piano. The call came on recommendation of bassist Steve Swallow, a former bandmate in Pete La Roca's quartet with John Gilmore. This specific group can be heard on the Pete La Roca recording *Turkish Women at the Bath*,[5] one of the few recordings that features John Gilmore outside of his duties with the Sun Ra Orchestra. Actually, without Steve's mentorship, the first recording of Corea's influential songs "Litha" and "Windows" might not have happened:

> The original group for *Sweet Rain* was Roy Haynes and Steve Swallow, but then Stan didn't want to use Roy on that gig for some reason, whatever, and because of that, Steve, in a group spirit, said,

> "well, I'm not going to be on the record either." So then, in a group spirit, I said, "Well, I'm not going to be on the record either." Then Steve called me up. He said, "No-no, Corea, you should go do that record. Stan is going to record some of your songs. This will be good for you."[6]

An even more important lesson while playing in Stan Getz's band was the leader's advice of limiting the soloing to two choruses and creating a message that's concise and lyrical. Initially Corea wasn't thinking about the need to fit in a group concept and often went into his own zone with elaborate piano introductions and extended solos. Stan's advice made him realize the importance of becoming a valuable group member by shaping his personal expression according to the group's concept and needs. The saxophonist modeled his masterful development of melodies drawing the listeners into the improvisational process on a nightly basis.

Word spread about Corea's sideman work and through a recommendation by Herbie Mickman, Sarah Vaughn's musical director, he became a member of her group from 1966 to 1968. On the side, he also frequently performed with Herbie Mann's group, among others. The flutist was not only a successful bandleader but also an entrepreneur who decided to start his own record company, the Vortex label. He invited Corea to do a recording for the label. Corea brought his rehearsal band with Steve Swallow, Joe Farrell, Joe Chambers, and Woody Shaw to the Atlantic Studios in New York City for his first recording as a leader. *Tones for Joan's Bones* featured three of Corea's original compositions: "Litha," "Tones for Joan's Bones," and "Straight Up and Down," as well as Kurt Weill's "This Is New."[7] The 1967 release on the Atlantic/Vortex label received a glowing 4.5-star review in *DownBeat* magazine and is a strong documentation of Corea's evolving style and his masterful compositions. Reviewer Harvey Pekar provided a glimpse of things to come when he mentioned:

> Here's a real sleeper. Corea and his sidemen are not among the most well-known performers in jazz, but they've cut a splendid record. . . . Incidentally, it wouldn't be a bad idea if the trio of Corea, Swallow and Chambers were given the opportunity to make an LP by themselves.[8]

Much experimentation was going on during the 1960s as jazz musicians were pushing traditional boundaries parallel to the quest for freedom during the civil rights movement. Recordings by Ornette Coleman, John Coltrane, Charles Mingus, Cecil Taylor, Albert Ayler, Eric Dolphy, and many more explored pure forms of musical expression beyond the limitations of harmonies, modes, and rhythm.[9] When the label Solid State offered Corea the opportunity to lead a trio recording in 1968, he asked bassist Miroslav Vitous and drummer Roy Haynes, both known for their experimental work, to join him. It proved to be a fortuitous combination of like minds, and after three days of recording first takes only at A&R Studios in New York, *Now He Sings, Now He Sobs* (Solid State SR 3157, 1968) was destined to become one of the most influential jazz trio recordings in history. Enjoy a glimpse into the studio during these historical sessions at the end of this chapter.

By the end of his first decade on the New York scene, Corea had certainly paid his dues and one of the people who took notice of his work was famed trumpeter Miles Davis. Always on the lookout for exciting young players, Miles frequented the clubs such as Birdland and the legendary jam sessions at Minton's Playhouse. The call came from his young drum prodigy Tony Williams: "Miles wants you to come to Baltimore. Herbie can't make it." Miles was looking for a new sound, a change in direction, and when the Fender Rhodes electric piano appeared on the scene only six months later, it opened the doors to the exciting new combination of electronic sounds with rock grooves and jazz sensibilities soon to be known as fusion.

LET'S TAKE A LISTEN TO "CHICK'S TUNE" (CHICK COREA)

From *The Thing to Do*, Blue Note BST 84178, recorded at Van Gelder Studio, Englewood Cliffs, NJ, July 30, 1964, with Blue Mitchell (trumpet), Junior Cook (tenor saxophone), Chick Corea (piano), Gene Taylor (bass), Al Foster (drums)

It's July 1964 and we get to listen in on Chick Corea's first recording session at the legendary Van Gelder Studio for Blue Note Records. It is a very exciting moment for Corea since the leader of the group, Richard Allen "Blue" Mitchell (1930–1979), saxophonist Junior Cook, and bassist Gene Taylor have been members of legendary pianist Horace Silver's group for the past six years. Corea has studied many of Silver's tunes and copied his piano solos as a teenager[10] as he admires his hard-grooving style. Now he has the opportunity to be the pianist with Silver's group and a new talented twenty-one-year-old drummer on the New York scene named Al Foster. The group has just completed a string of six performance dates playing their new repertoire as Blue Mitchell wanted to bring a well-rehearsed group to this recording date, just as his mentor Horace Silver had taught him. The repertoire includes five songs: "Fungii Mama" by Mitchell himself, "Mona's Mood" and "The Thing to Do" by Jimmy Heather, "Step Lightly" by Joe Henderson, and finally Chick Corea's first original to be recorded with the very simple title "Chick's Tune."

It's finally time for a take of "Chick's Tune," and the group decides to feature Al Foster with an 8-bar drum introduction. It'll be the last selection on the record so a little texture change seems appropriate. He ends his energetic solo with a hit and the band comes in with the Latin-tinged melody. As we listen to the melody unfold, we realize that there is something very familiar about the harmonic progression of this tune. During the previous two decades, as bebop musicians developed a more sophisticated melodic language, they often used familiar harmonic vehicles as a point of departure. A harmonic progression of a well-known standard would be played with a new original melody and the result is called a "contrafact," similar to the common 12-bar blues progression being used for countless blues songs. Thus, musicians are immediately familiar with the tune and comfortable improvising and labels won't have to deal with royalty distributions to outside composers. Now we recognize it: "Chick's Tune" is a contrafact on the standard "You Stepped Out of a Dream," a song composed in 1940 by Nacio Herb Brown with lyrics by Gus Kahn. It became popular in 1941, the year Chick was born, in the musical film *Ziegfeld Girl* featuring among others Judy Garland, Hedy Lamarr, and Lana Turner as three showbiz girls. What a fun coincidence that Corea chose this song as the harmonic vehicle for the "birth" of his recording career. It's also a quite unusual chord progression for a standard with some unexpected key changes, possibly simulating the process of waking up, that is, stepping out of a dream. After the first two measures in C major, the key shifts up a half step to D-flat major for the next two measures. Corea's new melody for the song sounds like a wake-up call jumping up and down with large skips over the two very distinct major scales. Then Al digs in and bassist Gene Taylor starts walking as they change into a swing groove for the fifth bar and yet another tonality change to A-flat major. Now the horns and piano break into triad harmonies, while the bass and drums play repeated notes on beats two and four, a technique called pedal point. This is a bit of an alteration from the original chord progression, which moves to yet another key before cycling back to C. The second half of the song starts with the same wake-up call and the half-step move followed by four bars of hard-grooving swing. Then bass, drums, and piano hit together at the end of the four bars and let the horns play a triplet sequence in harmony for two measures before they rejoin to swing into a turnaround and right into Corea's piano solo. What an honor for him to get the first solo, which is usually claimed by one of the horn players.

Corea takes a breath for the first two bars, then starts with a careful back-and-forth sequence before he takes off swinging hard with Gene and Al. His lines get busier and higher especially as he moves into the third chorus. Some Monkish dissonances, hitting two consecutive keys at the same time, create tension throughout chorus four. We can hear him explore the sound of some of the new scales popularized by the bebop innovators, such as the whole-tone scale[11] as well as creative rhythmic ideas before he winds down with some traditional block chords in George Shearing fashion. What a confident statement and glimpse of things to come on this very first Blue Note date!

Now it's Junior Cook's turn on the saxophone. He picks right up on the first beat of the chorus and the rhythm section is on fire. The energy drives him through four masterful choruses, taking the lead from Corea in terms of length and excitement. Junior concludes with a G-major triad played backwards right at the beginning of the new chorus and Blue responds to the call immediately with the same idea adapted to the half-step key change. We're now more than five minutes into the recording; this might be the final take! Crisp, lyrical lines unfold, while the rhythm section swings along, complementing with piano chords and accents. Blue's trumpet sound is strong and beautiful as always and he easily fills his four choruses with creative melodic ideas. As is customary after the conclusion of the individual solos, Junior initiates a segment of trading fills with the drummer. He takes the first eight bars of the chorus, while the drummer fills in the next eight bars. Next up is Blue for eight, and Al is back with more fills. His rolls are powerful and relentless as the same sequence repeats, the horns respond to his rhythms—this is not the time to lose any energy.

It's time to play the melody one last time with the switches between Latin and swing rhythms. With all the excitement, the tempo has picked up slightly; it's a very powerful take. The trumpet takes the melody an octave up for the last few notes, one last drum fill for two measures, and everyone joins on the last note, releasing the tension in flourishes and fills and one last cymbal crash. This is it—Blue Mitchell has established his career as a leader and Chick Corea has made his recording debut.

LET'S TAKE A LISTEN TO "MATRIX" (CHICK COREA)

From *Now He Sings, Now He Sobs*, Blue Note CDP 7900552, recorded at A&R Studios, New York, March 14, 19, and 27, 1968, with Chick Corea (piano), Miroslav Vitous (bass), Roy Haynes (drums)

The year 1968 is full of political turmoil. The Vietnam War is heading toward disaster as President Lyndon Johnson announces his decision not to run for reelection. Martin Luther King Jr. leads protest marches in his fight to bring people together in peace and righteousness. On March 14, we're entering the A&R Studios in New York City with a trio of young musicians ready to record their first album under Chick Corea's leadership for Solid State, a label soon to be bought by the legendary Blue Note Records label. For the past four years, Chick has played and recorded with various groups and players. He invited bassist Miroslav Vitous, whom he had played with in Donald Byrd's group, and drummer Roy Haynes, his bandmate with Stan Getz, to form the inaugural Chick Corea Trio ready to record *Now He Sings, Now He Sobs*, one of the most influential modern jazz albums. Later in an interview for *Piano & Keyboard* magazine, he explains his reasoning for choosing his collaborators:

> I think I used a bit of the idea that later on I noticed Miles would use. It's not such an unusual thing for a musician to do, especially in improvised music—to choose your partners as a priority over choosing your music.[12]

Thus the trio is quite enthusiastic about this recording opportunity, but there hasn't been much preparation of repertoire and rehearsal. For the song "Matrix," Corea offers a skeleton melody based on a 12-bar blues form. The melody is quite unusual for a blues tune as it does not use the regular blues scale with its minor sound and dissonant notes but rather walks up the major scale with triad patterns moving up stepwise for the first four bars (each four beats long), then we get a diminished sounding fill for the next four bars and back to the major scale pattern, this time descending stepwise down the scale for the last four bars of the blues form. As is common for a blues, this melody is repeated with subtle variations.

Now Corea embarks on a powerful 16-chorus solo—each chorus completes one 12-bar blues cycle. Miroslav and Roy are listening closely as Corea unfolds his extensive melodic repertoire and respond with great intuition and support of mood and musical tension. Right at the beginning of his solo, Corea clearly sets the tone for a new melodic language that uses extended lines, often more than six bars long, with patterns based on pentatonic scales (the first three and fifth and sixth note of a major scale). Thus even though the harmonies follow the blues form, the unusual melodic choices and extended lines make it difficult to follow the blues choruses. As Corea enters his second chorus, he uses another modern technique called sideslipping. He plays a descending four-note pattern using a pentatonic scale that's a half step too high and then resolves it to the natural pattern in the fourth bar of the chorus. As a result the listener perks up and feels the tension due to the sharpness of the sound and relief as the melodies synchronize again with the harmonies. As the solo unfolds, Corea builds on a mix of those techniques with the occasional bluesy note thrown in while Miroslav walks in quarter notes on the bass at a breakneck tempo. Roy keeps a swing beat with accents following Corea's rhythms and phrases as quickly as he can recognize his thoughts.

After Corea winds down the exciting solo journey with a series of rhythmic piano chords, Miroslav takes an unaccompanied bass solo for seven choruses. He gets to display his virtuosity on the bass with a mix of melodic patterns, adding some low notes underneath, and brings everyone back by starting to "walk" in quarter notes. The excitement builds back up with a trading section between piano and drums where each take turns on a 12-bar chorus. This exchange is very similar to a conversation as both respond to rhythms and patterns in the other's solos while adding new ideas. After the fourth exchange, Corea adds one last solo chorus and then goes back to the initial repeated melody based on the ascending and descending major scale movement. The tension is released with some piano tingles and drum rolls, and it's easy to imagine them getting up from their instruments and complimenting each other on a successful take for the album. Everything is recorded directly to two-track analog tape with no subsequent mixing and overdubbed tracks—thus we get the pure joy, excitement, and high level of artistry of these three musicians as they create this enduring masterpiece.

2

BITCHES BREW AND *IN A SILENT WAY*

The year 1968 is a year of turmoil, progress, and change. The Vietnam War and civil rights movement create tension, which escalates with the assassination of Martin Luther King Jr. on April 4. America and Russia race to get to the moon, with only a few more months to go until Neil Armstrong firmly places the American flag on lunar soil. President Nixon takes the lead for the next four years—the same period that brings Chick Corea to international stardom. This is also the year where he will discover L. Ron Hubbard's Scientology and his philosophy of communication and the new electronic sounds of the Fender Rhodes.

Months after recording *Now He Sings, Now He Sobs*, Corea replaced Herbie Hancock in Miles Davis's band. Inspired by the grooves and use of electronic instruments of funk groups such as Sly and the Family Stone, Davis experimented with a fusion of jazz, funk, and rock elements. The year 1968 was also the year when Davis's wife Betty Mabry introduced him to guitarist Jimi Hendrix. For the recording of *In a Silent Way* and *Bitches Brew* in 1969, he assembled a crop of young jazz artists willing to collaborate in a new way with sparse compositional frameworks, a variety of electronic instruments such as the Fender Rhodes electric piano, and extended jamming.

The sessions not only became the big bang of jazz rock, but also inspired future fusion pioneers and band members Chick Corea, Joe Zawinul, Herbie Hancock, John McLaughlin, Tony Williams, and Larry White to experiment with their own combination of styles and group formats. The new developments were part of a larger paradigm shift with a cultural context that encouraged experimentation with new styles, sounds, and recording techniques. As early as 1962 British pianist/guitarist Alexis Korner experimented with a mix of electric blues and R&B music in his group *Blues Incorporated.* Future luminaries like guitarist John McLaughlin who would soon join Miles Davis's new group in the United States, Mick Jagger, and drummer Ginger Baker passed through Korner's band.[1] He liked to surround himself with jazz musicians and often included horn sections in his groups. Rumor has it that Jimmy Page found out about a new singer called Robert Plant through his collaboration with Korner and asked Plant to join his group the New Yardbirds, a.k.a. Led Zeppelin. Other prominent British groups in the sixties experimenting with the combination of jazz and rock were Colosseum, Soft Machine, Nucleus, Jethro Tull, and King Crimson.

In New York, a group of jazz musicians gathered regularly in 1965–1966 to expand their horizons and experiment with elements of rock music. Among them were guitarists Larry Coryell and Joe Beck, saxophonists Jim Pepper and Charles Lloyd, and trumpeters Randy Brecker and Don Cherry. A variety of recorded collaborations are the results of their encounters. For example, Larry Coryell released a highly regarded album titled *Spaces*[2] in 1970 on the Vanguard label that featured fellow guitarist John McLaughlin, Chick Corea, bassist Miroslav Vitous, and drummer Billy Cobham. Both John McLaughlin and Chick Corea were members of Miles Davis's band during the *Bitches Brew* sessions, Miroslav Vitous was the bassist on Chick Corea's groundbreaking trio recording *Now He Sings, Now He Sobs*[3] as discussed during the last chapter, and drummer Billy Cobham played with guitarist John Abercrombie before joining John McLaughlin's Mahavishnu Orchestra in 1971.

Another example is drummer Tony Williams's band Lifetime, featuring guitarist John McLaughlin and organist Larry Young. In May of 1969, they released a jazz-rock album titled *Emergency*[4] on the Polydor label. Tony Williams had joined the Miles Davis Quintet in 1963 when he was only seventeen years old and released his first album as a leader, *Life Time*, just a year later. Williams's inventive playing redefined the role of the rhythm section in jazz and the blossoming jazz-rock movement with his polyrhythmic playing and changing meters.

During the same period, many American rock bands incorporated touches of free jazz and psychedelic-sounding improvisations into their live shows. Forever associated with the summer of love, 1967, the Grateful Dead became a social institution with their energetic and spontaneous live act.[5] Around the same time the Byrds and Jefferson Airplane incorporated heavier doses of improvisation after the success of Jimmy Hendrix and British supergroup Cream. Horn-based rock bands such as Blood, Sweat & Tears and Chicago featured jazz elements in their arranging techniques, and guitarist Carlos Santana blended Latin sounds with rock and jazz. But the main influences of Chick Corea's new employer, Miles Davis, were the grooves and popular success of Sly and the Family Stone, Jimi Hendrix, and James Brown.

During the summer of 1968, Miles led two recording sessions for Columbia Records. The first session took place June 19–21 at Columbia's 30th Street Studio featuring his "Second Great Quintet" with Wayne Shorter on saxophone, Herbie Hancock on keys, Ron Carter on bass, and Tony Williams on drums. It marked Davis's departure from the traditional jazz sound to experimentations with electronic keyboards and bass as well as free forms with vamp-like structures and a variety of grooves. Instead of focusing on creating melodies on existing chord structures, the focus shifted to groove experimentations with melodic fragments as afterthoughts.[6] During a second session on September 24, 1968, Chick Corea replaced Herbie Hancock and bassist Dave Holland replaced Ron Carter for the recording of two additional tracks, "Frelon Brun" and "Mademoiselle Mabry," thus effectively breaking up his regular group. The result of the two sessions, the 1968 release *Filles de Kilimanjaro*, receives extremely positive reviews with five stars in *DownBeat* magazine as well as the *Rolling Stone Jazz Record Guide*. The recording marks the transition to Miles's electric period starting with the release of *In a Silent Way* in 1969 and *Bitches Brew* in 1970. In fact, the tribute piece to his brand-new wife Betty Mabry, "Mademoiselle Mabry," is a reharmonization of Jimi Hendrix's "Wind Cries Mary."

After more experimentation with personnel and sound, Miles had a plan. On February 18, 1969, he assembled a group of four of his live band members: Chick Corea, Wayne Shorter, Dave Holland, and himself, and added two more keyboard players with Joe Zawinul and Herbie Hancock, as well as drummer Tony Williams and British guitarist John McLaughlin, for the legendary Columbia session on February 18, 1969, that led to the release of *In a Silent Way*.[7] Joe Zawinul brought the title tune to the studio, which Miles proceeded to reinvent by changing the harmonies and picking out melodic fragments. Throughout the session, Miles guided the players toward experimentation by asking John McLaughlin to play as if he were rediscovering the guitar and by giving minimal directions during the first readings of the disassembled tunes, which ended up as the master takes to the surprise of all players. Producer Teo Macero heavily edited the recorded tracks by selecting various segments and splicing them together in new ways, a technique unheard of for jazz recordings. The result was an ambient album with rock grooves and jazz improvisations that some called a "tone poem," some called "droning wallpaper music"; it certainly was a completely new approach.[8] Furthermore, it is notable that in addition to its innovative impact *In a Silent Way* also achieved outstanding commercial success. It reached No. 134 on the Billboard 200, No. 40 in R& B Albums, and No. 3 on the Jazz charts.

Just weeks after the release of *In a Silent Way*, Miles summoned his live band and additional players back into the studio, ready to brew up a mix of about every musical polarity of the sixties into arguably the most revolutionary jazz album in history: *Bitches Brew*.[9] The sessions started at 10:00 a.m. on Tuesday, August 19, 1969, and for the next three days, sorcerer Miles brewed up blocks of sounds and grooves with three keyboards, two drums, electric and acoustic bass, percussion, guitar, soprano sax, trumpet, and bass clarinet. Producer Teo Macero spliced and reassembled the blocks, and with liner notes by Ralph Gleason, the results were packaged with an eye-catching cover painted in a stylistic mix of surrealism and pop culture by Mati Klarwein under a hip title. *Bitches Brew*[10] was released in April 1970, sold four hundred thousand copies during its first year, and earned Miles Davis a Grammy Award for Best Jazz Performance, Soloist with Large Group. Get an inside view of the studio sessions in the listening guide for the title track at the end of this chapter.

Throughout their time as members of Miles Davis's band, Chick Corea and bassist Dave Holland had developed an affinity for playing freely together encouraged by the experimental spirit of the group. For months they rehearsed in Corea's Nineteenth Street loft as a duo until drummer Barry Altschul joined them. As it became clear that Miles had a new direction in mind that was increasingly rooted in rock rhythms, Corea and Holland decided to part ways with the group and pursue their own project.

LET'S TAKE A LISTEN TO "IN A SILENT WAY" (JOE ZAWINUL)

From *In a Silent Way*, Columbia 40580, released July 30, 1969, recorded February 18, 1969, at CBS 39th Street Studio B, New York, featuring Miles Davis (trumpet), Wayne Shorter (soprano sax), John McLaughlin (electric guitar), Chick Corea (electric piano), Herbie Hancock (electric piano), Joe Zawinul (organ), Dave Holland (bass), Tony Williams (drums)

Twenty-one-year-old reviewer Lester Bangs for *Rolling Stone* magazine wrote this glowing review published on November 15, 1969:

> Side two opens and closes with the best song on the album, a timeless trumpet prayer called "In a Silent Way." There has always been something eternal and pure in Miles' music, and this piece captures that quality as well as anything he's ever recorded. If, as I believe, Miles is an artist for the ages, then this piece will be among those that stand through those vast tracks of time to remind future generations of the oneness of human experience.

"In a Silent Way" is the title track of *In a Silent Way* released on Columbia Records July 30, 1969. The four-minute edited piece opens and closes the second LP side with "It's about That Time" between the two segments. Miles Davis was on a mission—rock music was taking over, he witnessed the popularity and loved the groove of Sly and the Family Stone, and his new wife Betty Mabry had just introduced him to the young guitar phenomenon Jimi Hendrix.

In the morning of February 18, 1969, Miles called keyboardist Joe Zawinul and casually invited him for a recording session. Just a few minutes later he called again with the instructions "Bring some music."[11] Joe Zawinul obliged and brought several selections, among them a lead sheet for "In a Silent Way." As soon as everyone had arrived in the studio, they started rehearsing. Besides the regular quintet with

Miles Davis on trumpet, Wayne Shorter on soprano sax, Chick Corea on keyboards, Dave Holland on bass, and Tony Williams on drums, Miles had invited three more guest performers: Joe Zawinul on organ, Herbie Hancock on keyboards, and English guitarist John McLaughlin who had just arrived in the United States two weeks earlier on the invitation of drummer Tony Williams. Adding new players to a group on the recording date is a very unusual strategy as it adds uncertainty to the players and the performance. But that was exactly Miles's intention, a certain element of unease and heightened concentration.

The group ran through "In a Silent Way," and it was obvious that Miles wasn't happy. He grabbed the music and eliminated all the chords, leaving a bare skeleton of melodies. Then, to the great surprise of the musicians, he asked them to just play off the melodies. Corea recalls: "His genius as a bandleader was in his group way of thinking, and in choosing the musicians and leading them forward by what he played, and by the way he used the ideas he or someone else brought to the band."[12]

It was time to record, and just as the tape started rolling, Miles turned to a nervous John McLaughlin and told him to play the guitar like he didn't know how to play it. McLaughlin, who had made a name for himself in England for his advanced virtuosity, held back and played the melody in a very tentative, exploratory fashion. Every note is clearly and slowly articulated as if the guitarist is asking for confirmation from the bandleader and his fellow musicians. Then Wayne Shorter takes over the melody in a similar exploratory and tentative fashion. The keyboardists create colorful textures, carefully listening to each other and to the lead instruments in order to match harmonies and support the melodies. Finally Miles joins on the melody, doubling Wayne Shorter's soprano sax. The musicians finish the take with the exploratory, searching attitude thinking that this was the tryout for the real recording. To everyone's surprise, this ended up being the master take. "You never knew what was going to happen, so there was always an edge of nervousness. That's the way he pulled things out of you," recalls John McLaughlin.[13]

Similar to what producer George Martin ended up being for the Beatles, producer Teo Macero became for Miles Davis for this session and subsequent recordings for the next six years. By working with looping and editing, Macero assembled a collage of pieces emulating the classical sonata form on both sides of the LP. For the tune "In a Silent Way," he took four minutes of the initial recording, then edited in an eleven-minute companion track, "It's about That Time," and used the same four minutes from "In a Silent Way" to close out the 19:53 track taking up the complete second LP side. What seems to be a pretty common editing technique now was quite involved in 1969 as digital recording and "cut and paste" was not available yet. Macero had to carefully splice the tape with a razor blade and a good ear, and with lots of patience reassemble the pieces to achieve smooth transitions and the intended effect. The middle piece, "It's about That Time," is based on a bass vamp and features solos by Miles, McLaughlin, and Shorter in the spirit of mashing jazz and rock inspired by Miles's inspirations from Jimi Hendrix and Sly and the Family Stone.

The concept of looping and repeating segments of the recording session was quite revolutionary for jazz. In addition, the use of rock grooves and electronic instruments was controversial at the time even in contemporary jazz. The album was visionary and ahead of its time and it is surprising how well the public responded to it. The album peaked at No. 134 on the Billboard Top LPs chart and thus became Miles's first album in four years, since *My Funny Valentine*, to reach the charts—a sign of things to come!

LET'S TAKE A LISTEN TO "BITCHES BREW"

From *Bitches Brew*, Columbia 40580, released April 1970, recorded August 19–21, 1969, at CBS 39th Street Studio B, New York, featuring Miles Davis (trumpet), Wayne Shorter (soprano sax), Bennie Maupin (bass clarinet), John McLaughlin (electric guitar), Chick Corea (electric piano), Joe Zawinul (electric piano), Dave Holland (bass), Harvey Brooks (electric bass), Lenny White (drums), Jack DeJohnette (drums), Don Alias (congas), Juma Santos (shaker)

Tuesday, August 19, 1969, was a hot summer day in New York. By 10:00 a.m. Columbia Studio B was crowded with twelve musicians, producer Teo Macero, and engineer Stan Tonkel. With two drummers, two bassists, and two keyboard players performing simultaneously, there were not enough booths in the studio to isolate each player and get individual sounds. Headphones and monitor mixes were largely ignored, and with little instruction and only some compositional sketches the musicians started exploring sounds and grooves. The tape was rolling from the start on Miles's request. Similar to the *In a Silent Way* sessions earlier that year, Miles had assembled his regular live group with Wayne Shorter, Chick Corea, and Dave Holland, but also invited a host of guest musicians whom he had scouted at jam sessions and through recommendations. Drummer Lenny White, who was only nineteen at the time, recalls the following setup: "We were all set up in a semi-circle with Miles in the center. He had a tall music stand and he conducted everything. All the sessions in August 1969 started at 10 in the morning and lasted until 1 or 2 in the afternoon."[14]

The album *In a Silent Way* had just been released two weeks earlier and Miles had been performing frequently with his current group. He was in top form and he was on a mission. The favorable audience reception of *In a Silent Way* seemed to indicate that the world was ready for his concept of fusing elements of jazz and rock with current technological advances such as electronic keyboards and tape editing and looping. He brought musical sketches to the studio and had rehearsed some ideas and themes, but the goal was to capture the encounter of these twelve musicians as they engaged in exploratory improvisations with minimal given structures.

The first tune captured on tape that Tuesday was "Bitches Brew." Originally conceived as a five-part suite, only three sections were recorded and two ended up on the master spliced together, one as the intro/interlude/coda and the other one as a repeated bass vamp for the solos. The track starts with repeated bass notes interrupted by percussive chords on the Fender Rhodes. Miles enters after forty seconds with a short motif and a high bend distorted by an echo effect. Saxophonist Wayne Shorter recalls that Miles was playing off lyrics written by his wife, Betty Mabry, to a song called "I'm a Down Home Girl." She actually attended the session and Shorter called it "an emotional hook."[15] The trumpet section with the echo effect is looped five times in five- to ten-second intervals until section 2 kicks in with Bennie Maupin grooving on the bass clarinet. Miles takes the first solo. Just a month earlier "Spinning Wheel," a new single by the rock group Blood, Sweat & Tears, had reached No. 2 on the Billboard charts and would be nominated for three Grammys at the 1970 ceremony, winning the Grammy for Best Instrumental Arrangement. Inspired by the new radio hit, Miles's solo seems like a psychedelic parody of "Spinning Wheel" with recurring fragments of the melody. At 6:32 John McLaughlin takes the tentative lead on guitar. Miles is back at 8:55 and there is the "Spinning Wheel" suggestion again. After a short saxophone solo by Wayne Shorter, Chick Corea gets his turn on the Fender Rhodes keyboard. With fragmented chord patterns and short melodic phrases, Chick paints a sonic landscape for us that accents the ongoing groove by the rhythm section. At 14:36 we hear the familiar emotional trumpet hook with the echo effect again—producer Teo Macero spliced it in here as an interlude. The bass clarinet groove returns and after one last trumpet solo before the original intro gets spliced back in as the coda section and concludes this nearly twenty-seven-minute track. None of the musicians in the studio could have imagined the final shape of the music after Macero's extensive tape looping and splicing—a true revolution for jazz as a musical style—making *Bitches Brew* arguably "The Most Revolutionary Jazz Album in History."[16]

3

CIRCLE—AN AVANT-GARDE EXCURSION

In mid-August 1959, the Lenox School of Jazz was in full session at the Music Inn in Lenox, Massachusetts, close to Tanglewood, the summer home of the Boston Symphony Orchestra, bringing together for the third time prominent jazz scholars and performers with forty-five selected students from all over the world. The principle of teaching jazz in an academic setting was quite new and the structure of the curriculum experimental. Lectures might detour into lengthy and heated theory discussions. But when a young alto saxophonist from Texas, Ornette Coleman, arrived at the camp sponsored by John Lewis from the Modern Jazz Quartet, his radical ideas caused a split into two camps of faculty holding opposing views on the value of the avant-garde.[1] Larry Ridley, a young bassist from Indianapolis, played in Coleman's combo that summer and remembers the confusion caused by the novel approach: "And Ornette used to say, 'Just play what you hear and what you feel.' And he gave me this music to read with no bar lines. I'm saying, 'Wait a minute, Ornette, what's happening here? There are no bar lines.' And he says, 'Oh, just play it.'"[2]

Just a few months later, Ornette presented his new ideas with a double quartet (two drummers, two bassists, two trumpets, and two saxophones) in New York at the Five Spot jazz club. His principles were based on improvising on the feeling and inspiration of a song rather than on the chord structure. For this group he eliminated all harmony instruments such as the piano or guitar in order to achieve maximum freedom. His close collaborator, bassist Charlie Haden, explains that the spirit of the music is to play and improvise with an energy that's going to change the world.[3] Coleman's 1960 recording for Atlantic Records titled *Free Jazz: A Collective Improvisation* achieved that goal.[4] The album served as one of the models for a free collaborative jazz style popular especially during the 1960s and early '70s and commonly referred to as free jazz.

Throughout his early time in New York, Chick Corea eagerly assimilated the explorations of the avant-garde. When he became a member of Miles Davis's "Third Great Quintet" with Wayne Shorter on saxophone, Miles Davis, bassist David Holland, and drummer Jack DeJohnette often augmented by percussionist Airto Moreira from 1968 to 1970, Corea was able to experiment with free improvisation as the group stretched song forms beyond limits and built long collaborative segments on minimal structures.[5] Unfortunately, this specific group was never officially recorded and can only be heard as part of the *In a Silent Way* and *Bitches Brew* sessions discussed in the previous chapter. Limited editions of live footage have been released over the years with the bootleg recording *Live at the Fillmore East March 7, 1970: It's about That Time*[6] showcasing some of the best moments of this particular quintet. Corea displays a dazzling amount of virtuosity and density of ideas during the concert while Holland and DeJohnette provide electrifying grooves for Miles Davis's and Wayne Shorter's extended and high-energy solos.

Later that same year, Chick Corea and David Holland decided to leave Davis's group and lead their own acoustic collaboration as they had formed a close improvisational bond during the live performances as well as many hours of private loft jamming. They found a like-minded collaborator with drummer Barry Altschul pushing the piano trio format into the outer realms of abstraction. The special chemistry between Corea and Holland had already been captured during a three-day recording session in 1969 with current Miles Davis drummer Jack DeJohnette, Woody Shaw on trumpet, Bennie Maupin on bass clarinet, and Hubert Laws on flute. Thom Jurek describes it in an AllMusic review[7] as "out jazz that any jazz fan can appreciate." The sessions were originally released as two different recordings: *IS* on Solid State and *Sundance* on Groove Merchant.[8]

The group Circle expanded to a quartet with the addition of Anthony Braxton on saxophone and started touring internationally as well as recorded a series of sessions for Blue Note Records in 1970, later released as double LPs *Circling In* and *Circulus* in 1975 and 1978, respectively. The group also caught the attention of German producer Manfred Eicher, who had just founded a new record label called Editions of Contemporary Music (ECM) dedicated to presenting jazz with a chamber music concept and an approach that was different from the popular American jazz labels Blue Note and Impulse. Eicher explains: "I wanted to record more as if it were chamber music, with more detail, more focus on the overtones to give an impression of air in the music, like you get in a concert hall or church."[9] As a production assistant for Deutsche Grammophon, Eicher had already met many of the current New York musicians and when the owner of a Munich record shop offered him money to make some recordings, he called his favorite pianists: Mal Waldron, Paul Bley, Chick Corea, and Keith Jarrett. His approach to picking unique artists and creating crystal-clear and meticulously balanced recordings packaged in abstract designs and photographs of landscapes rather than the typical artist head shots changed the concept of jazz recordings for decades to come.[10]

The trio of Corea, Holland, and Altschul recorded during January 1971 at the new studio home of ECM Records, Bauer Studios in Ludwigsburg, Germany, capturing their intricate and free interactions.[11] Just a month later, a live set of the group Circle in Paris with the addition of Anthony Braxton was captured and released as the double LP *Live in Paris* (ECM 1018/19). Scott Yanow assigned five stars to the recording and wrote in his *All Music Guide* review: "The music is often quite abstract but generally colorful and innovative and this set remains one of the high points of Corea's productive career."[12] One of the songs that appears on several recordings and was a frequent feature of Circle's live repertoire is Wayne Shorter's "Nefertiti." See the listening guide at the end of this chapter for a glimpse into the collaborative nature and avant-garde style of the group.

Just a few months later, Corea broke up Circle with little advance notice. After recording a series of solo piano improvisations he founded a new group featuring vocals and a melodic fusion of Latin American music styles with jazz. The change in direction seemed sudden and he later explained: "When I see an artist using his energies and technique to create a music way beyond the ability of people to connect with it, I see his abilities being wasted." In the same interview Chick mentioned:

"But the reason I left Circle and wanted to do something else was basically to achieve a better balance between technique and communication, and to bring in the idea of communicating with the audience."[13] The abrupt change and expressed need for strong connection and communication with the audience coincides with Corea's discovery of Scientology in 1971, a cult that he has been associated with ever since.

Chick Corea is in illustrious company as a follower of Scientology—fellow members include film stars Tom Cruise, Nicole Kidman, Kirstie Alley, John Travolta, and Priscilla Presley and musicians Isaac Hayes, Edgar Winter, and Mark Isham, among others. The cult is based on the writings of science fiction author L. Ron Hubbard and his theory of Dianetics. Through a series of progressive courses, participants can clear themselves of "engrams" and achieve a higher level of control of their emotions and actions. "Engrams" refer to unconscious memories of pain triggered by a series of associations that can cause irrational behavior. Through a process called "auditing," these "engrams" can be made conscious and subsequently cleared. The goal is to achieve increasing levels of "clear" that allow the release of all physical and emotional pain and complete control of the mind on any decisions.

Corea has become a lifelong member of Scientology and believes that the system has helped him reach his fullest potential. In an interview with Philip Booth he explains: "The question of who we are and what we can do and what our potentials are and what is the mind and what is the body can be addressed. They can be talked about, and they can be discovered. They can be answered. And with those answers and data that you get to experience by looking into the area you can make advances."[14]

Since Scientology is focused on the psychological process of achieving a "clearer" state of mind rather than the teaching of a higher being, it is often categorized as a cult rather than a religion. Thus, laws allowing religious freedom do not apply and cults are banned for their manipulative nature, as is the case in Germany. When Chick Corea was initially hired to perform for the 1993 Athletic Championships in Stuttgart, Germany, the government canceled the contract based on his association with Scientology, an illegal cult in Germany, and the fact that this specific event was sponsored by the German government. Two lawsuits against the government's ruling by Corea's team were dismissed. Of course, Corea is allowed to perform concerts in Germany;

this ruling only applies to specifically government-sponsored contracts.[15]

In any case, a change in direction and musical approach is clearly noticeable after Corea's breakup of the group Circle. In April 1971, he recorded hours of solo piano music at the Arne Bendiksen Studio in Oslo, Norway, that resulted in two LP releases: *Piano Improvisations Volume 1 & 2* (ECM 1014). Especially volume 1 documents the evolution of a compositional approach that combines jazz with Latin rhythms and a touch of European classicism soon to become the trademark of Corea's most popular group, Return to Forever. The music received glowing reviews—Michael Cuscuna writes in *DownBeat* magazine: "His work there is truly beyond words. This is one of the most important piano albums I have heard." A book of Bill Dobbins's transcriptions of the music is available through Advance Music, and Dobbins mentions in his foreword: "Chick Corea's Piano Improvisations recordings for the ECM label have been highly influential in the evolution of the solo jazz piano tradition since the early 1970s. Along with solo recordings by Keith Jarrett and Paul Bley, they inspired a renewed interest in the art of solo piano improvising, which had been largely neglected since the era of Earl Hines, Fats Waller, Teddy Wilson and Art Tatum."[16] Both albums were released in 1971, and volume 2 even features two short covers of Thelonious Monk's "Trinkle Tinkle" and Wayne Shorter's "Masqualero." The recordings are a dazzling display of virtuosity, styles, and creative approaches to piano playing with a healthy dose of beautiful melodies and percussive rhythms.

The foundations for Corea's new concept and quest for communication was now in place and one of the most successful jazz groups was ready to burst on the scene. Corea explains his artistic vision in a 1973 column in *DownBeat* magazine:

> So you see, the artist has a very important and a very great responsibility. For if he uses his art to promote false or bad things or a low way of living, and gets enough agreement on it, conditions will get worse. But the beauty of it is that the artist also can conceive of the most beautiful things, the most loving and free-flowing way of living, the most wondrous not-yet-created universes—and he can begin to live this and create his art and communicate it with these things in mind. And if he pays attention to all the aspects involved and develops his ability to communicate well, wonderful things can and will

happen—and conditions around us will improve and our environment will become safer and more beautiful. This is what true art can do, and there's nothing more fulfilling than doing that.

So let's do it.[17]

LET'S TAKE A LISTEN TO "NEFERTITI" (WAYNE SHORTER)

From *A.R.C.*, ECM 1009, recorded January 11–13, 1971, at Tonstudio Bauer, Ludwigsburg, Germany, featuring Chick Corea (piano), David Holland (bass), Barry Altschul (drums); producer—Manfred Eicher

Chick Corea and Dave Holland had toured and recorded with Miles Davis for about three years with great international success. They enjoyed their intimate interaction and free collaboration but did not agree with Davis's increasing focus on electronic instruments, rock grooves, and new tape editing techniques. Shortly after the release of *Bitches Brew* they decided to leave the band and pursue their own project. Drummer Barry Altschul turned out to be a great match for their avant-garde excursions, and when German producer Manfred Eicher called with the invitation to join his brand-new record label the timing was perfect. On January 11, the trio set up in Tonstudio Bauer in the south German town of Ludwigsburg. Manfred Eicher was experimenting with a new concept of capturing the sound of the piano and allowing for optimal musical freedom in the recording studio. Only after the trio felt absolutely comfortable with the setup and the piano sound rang crystal clear in the headphones did Eicher give the green light for recording.

Corea started an extended solo piano introduction on Wayne Shorter's composition "Nefertiti." Named after an Egyptian queen, whose famous bust was found in the workshop of sculptor Thutmose, the tune was a popular repertoire piece for avant-garde groups. The fragmented melody and nonfunctional harmonies with floating key centers allow for open improvisations based on melodic materials rather than harmonic progressions. In fact, for the initial recording of the tune as the title track of Davis's 1968 Columbia release *Nefertiti*,[18] the horns continuously loop the melody while the rhythm section improvises, thus reversing traditional roles. Clearly, Corea aims for a similar concept as he develops variations on the theme with virtuosic embellishments and ambiguous harmonies during a two-minute solo piano intro. Holland and Altschul join at 2:13 swinging in full force while Corea digs deeper into creative treatments of the melody. At 4:29 we can hear a final cascade of eight melody repetitions before he displays his virtuosity in full force carrying his bandmates along into increasingly free collaborations. Finally the tension releases at 6:34 and Holland takes over on the bass with a flourish of notes showcasing his variation ideas of the melody. The piano trails away and opens up space for free interaction between bass and drums. At 8:20 Corea starts a trading sequence and the interaction reaches a climax just before he returns to the melody at 9:00. Holland and Altschul immediately react by settling back into the initial swing groove, and together they conclude the last statement of the 16-bar form with a flurry of rolls and tone clusters.

The track is a testimonial for the intimacy and high level of interaction that the trio was able to achieve based on their collaborative trust as well as producer Manfred Eicher's ability to facilitate the highest level of musical creativity by eliminating any sound obstacles. By January 13, 1970, one of the most successful avant-garde trio recordings would be complete and become one of the cornerstones of the legendary ECM label.

4

RETURN TO FOREVER— THE ACOUSTIC YEARS

"I decided to put some group music together in 1971. So I started writing some music, and the first piece I wrote I entitled 'Return to Forever.' . . . I [had] totally re-evaluated my past. I started my life anew—totally anew. Musically my intentions were no longer to satisfy myself. I really wanted to connect with the world and make my music mean something to people. And 'forever' poetically means to me a very nice state of being where time is not a pressure and a person is really feeling himself. It's something we need to 'return' to."[1]

The group Return to Forever, whose self-titled debut release has become Corea's biggest-selling album to date, was inspired by Corea's admiration for Joni Mitchell, Stevie Wonder, and the Beatles, as well as Scientology founder L. Ron Hubbard's mantra: "When in doubt, communicate."[2] The music is best described as a mix of Latin and classical traditions featuring some of jazz's most melodic compositions. Corea's newfound quest for communication with audiences and discovery of Scientology were the main drivers for this quite radical and ultimately most successful change in musical direction.

Scientology leader Neville Potter became Corea's mentor in his journey toward a clear state of mind. The relationship grew into a creative partnership with Potter contributing lyrics to the first two Return to Forever recordings as well as taking on the role of manager for the group.[3] The initial incarnation of the group included Stanley Clarke on bass, Joe Farrell on flute and saxophone, Airto Moreira on drums and percussion, and Airto's wife Flora Purim on vocals. Airto and Flora were taking Scientology courses at the time and Stanley Clarke was a member of the cult until the 1980s, thus providing a conceptual unity for the music.

Stanley Clarke was only nineteen when he met Chick Corea. He grew up in Philadelphia studying violin and cello, then upright bass and bass guitar, and gathered his first performing experiences in some of Philly's funk groups. The British Invasion was in full swing and rock 'n' roll dominated the airwaves, hence the young bassist had grown up with an affinity for the new sounds and was ready to integrate some of those modern elements into his performance repertoire. Of course, having the opportunity to be in Horace Silver's group and playing on sessions with Joe Henderson and Pharoah Sanders when he first came to New York was a dream come true, but he was ready to explore new creative directions. He remembered in an article for *Jazzwise* magazine:[4]

> "When I first met Chick I was, what, 19 or 20. Chick filled in for our keyboard player. I'd heard of Chick and we clicked, man. He talked about his ideas much like mine. We'd grown up listening to Miles and Coltrane but also Hendrix and James Brown. So I had a mixed feeling about jazz. . . . Imagine, when I met Chick, here was a guy who's into reaching an audience without, hopefully, compromising the music. So we started playing together."

Clarke's jaw-dropping technique was the perfect match for the new group, and his slapping style on the bass became legendary.[5]

Saxophonist Joe Farrell, originally from Chicago, had been a staple of the New York scene since the mid-1950s. A longtime member of the Thad Jones–Mel Lewis Orchestra, he had also recorded with Maynard Ferguson, George Russell, Jaki Byard, Charles Mingus, and Elvin Jones, to name a few. In 1970 he brought together his fellow alumni from Miles Davis's *In a Silent Way* sessions for a quartet recording released on CTI Records. The lineup included guest John McLaughlin on guitar, Chick Corea on keyboards, Dave Holland on bass, and Jack DeJohnette on drums recorded at the legendary Van Gelder Studio in Englewood Cliffs, New Jersey, with producer Creed Taylor. The two Chick Corea originals featured on the recording, "Song of the Wind" and "Motion," document the stylistic transformation from the free-flowing music of Circle to the rich melodic music of Return to Forever. As a longtime collaborator, Farrell became the logical choice for the lead instrument in Corea's new band.

Shortly after moving to New York in 1967, the Brazilian-born vocalist Flora Purim went to one of bassist Walter Booker's after-hours jam sessions. Born to parents who were classical musicians, she had studied music all her life and honed her skills playing guitar and singing in the nightclubs of her hometown Rio de Janeiro and São Paulo. Even though her Russian father had forbidden her to study and listen to jazz, her mother loved Oscar Peterson and Errol Garner and played their recordings during the day when her father was gone. Purim loved the freedom of jazz and, equipped with a five-octave vocal range, decided on a career as a vocalist and immersed herself in the New York jazz scene. At this particular jam session Chick Corea was playing piano, Joe Chambers drums, and Walter Booker himself was on bass. Saxophonist Stan Getz was also present and when he heard Flora's beautiful rendition of Antonio Carlos Jobim's composition "How Insensitive" he immediately invited her for a European tour. And in 1970 when Corea formed Return to Forever he recalled her emotional interpretations and ability to scat and add wordless melodies and invited Flora to join Return to Forever. Incidentally, Flora's daughter Diana married Walter Booker's son Krishna in 1998.

When Flora Purim realized that Chick Corea was still looking for a percussionist, she recommended her husband, Airto Moreira. They had met in Brazil when she briefly studied percussion and Moreira had recently joined her in New York, immediately working with Miles Davis. He was an expert in Latin American percussion techniques and had previously traveled throughout Brazil collecting and studying more than 120 percussion instruments. Since his early days in New York with Mongo Santamaria and Willie Bobo, Corea had an affinity for Latin rhythms and he gladly invited Moreira to join the band.

The band debuted in New York's Village Vanguard in November 1971 for an audience of eighteen with a fresh repertoire that Corea had written for the group. But the performance schedule was empty for the following months and the group needed opportunities to develop the challenging new music. A friend told Corea that Stan Getz had a tour planned but needed a band. Corea called him up and said, "Stan, for a little bit extra money I'll sort of become musical director and I can propose Tony Williams on drums, Stanley Clarke on bass and Airto

Moreira on percussion. And I'll even play a little Fender Rhodes and I'll bring these compositions with me."[6] Getz liked the idea and took the band on the road and even in the studio. They recorded *Captain Marvel*, titled after one of Corea's compositions featured on the recording. In addition, different versions of "500 Miles High" and "La Fiesta" can be heard on this recording, two Corea compositions that became trademarks of the early Return to Forever repertoire. Thom Jurek writes in his *AllMusic* review of the album: "This band, combining as it did the restlessness of electric jazz with Getz's trademark stubbornness in adhering to those principles that made modern jazz so great, made for a tension that came pouring out of the speakers with great mutual respect shining forth from every cut—especially the steamy Latin-drenched title track. *Captain Marvel* is arguably the finest recording Getz made during the 1970s."[7]

Getz's band had an extended engagement at the Rainbow Grill in New York with Joao Gilberto as guest artist, and while playing with Getz by night, Corea took the band into the A&R Studios during the day in New York in February 1972. The result was the self-titled debut album *Return to Forever*[8] that included "La Fiesta" initially released in Europe only in 1972 followed by an American release in 1975 after the original band had already broken up. Ironically, the release of Getz's album *Captain Marvel* also got delayed by three years due to legal complications, so American audiences first experienced the Return to Forever sound with the second album of the group, *Light as a Feather*,[9] recorded in October 1972 in London and released on Polydor in 1973. Arguably Corea's most popular composition, "Spain," is the closing track of *Light as a Feather* and has become a standard of the worldwide jazz repertoire—see the listening guide at the end of this chapter. The album also won the Playboy Jazz Album of the Year award and peaked at No. 6 on the Billboard Jazz Album charts.

The dancing Brazilian rhythms, the melodic tunes played by virtuosic musicians, and the emotional charge of Purim's vocals attracted audiences worldwide, and the news about this exciting new band spread quickly. Bassist Stanley Clarke recalls: "It's funny, people knew about it in the States because it had been an import (it received only a European release). It had pockets of support but when we went to Japan we were like The Beatles. We were met at the airport by people with banners! I still have the pictures: it was a really cool thing and I realized then there was something important about that band."[10]

With all the accolades coming in for the new album and worldwide tours, the band was on a roll and seemed unstoppable. But Flora and Airto had just started a family; their daughter Diana Moreira was born on August 15, 1972. They were not available for extensive touring and started working on their own projects. Consequently they left Return to Forever in 1973. Corea and Clarke wanted to continue the band and Clarke recommended teaming up with drummer Lenny White, another alum of Miles Davis's band. They had a week booked at Todd Barkan's new purchase in San Francisco, the Keystone Korner jazz club, and decided to use the opportunity to audition potential new Return to Forever band members.

Simultaneous to Return to Forever's rise to success, another *Bitches Brew* alum, guitarist John McLaughlin, took the world by storm with the Mahavishnu Orchestra featuring a complex fusion of electric jazz and rock with Eastern and Indian influences. In fact, the group was featured during the opening ceremonies of the 1972 Olympics in Munich. Corea and Clarke decided that they wanted a piece of the rock action and put out the call that they were looking for a guitarist. Bill Connors lived in the San Francisco area and, encouraged by bassist Steve Swallow, he joined Corea's trio at the Keystone Korner for one of the nights. Connors had listened to John Coltrane's use of scales and "sheets of sounds" but was excited about Eric Clapton's blues attack and use of effects. His style fused these influences together, and Corea and Clarke had found their match. The next Return to Forever album *Hymn of the Seventh Galaxy* was going to be a radical departure into the amplified rock world and soon the band would find itself competing with popular rock bands such as Yes and Emerson, Lake, & Palmer.

LET'S TAKE A LISTEN TO "SOMETIME AGO"

From *Piano Improvisations Vol. 1*, ECM 1014, recorded April 21–22, 1971, at Arne Bendiksen Studio in Oslo, Norway, Chick Corea (piano)

A tumultuous decade of fighting for civil rights and freedom had come to an end. Mankind had just walked on the moon for the third time and students protested against the Vietnam War. Rather than the quest for individual expression, a sense of unity and balance marked the beginning of the 1970s. Chick Corea had discovered the writings of L. Ron Hubbard, which helped him formulate a new artistic philosophy by clearing his mind from distracting emotions and thoughts, especially during the process of artistic creation. The primary ingredients of this new concept were communication with audiences and an artistic obligation to share beauty toward a better future. When he entered the studio in Oslo, surrounded by a late winter landscape and quiet space, Corea made a conscious decision to change the direction of his musical approach. Recently, he had written a variety of musical vignettes inspired by his early love for Latin rhythms and with a strong melodic focus. The songs didn't have names yet and were released under titles such as "Song for Sally," "Noon Song," "Ballad for Anna," and "Song for the Wind" on the *Piano Improvisations* albums but would soon become essential repertoire tunes for the new band.

He sat down and began to play. Producer Manfred Eicher checked on the piano sound—as pure and clean as possible was his ideal—and the studio acoustics provided just the right amount of room reverb. Corea closed his eyes and started playing, rarely requesting any second takes, just focusing his mind on the process of making music with a newfound clarity from his recent explorations in Dianetics. After a few tracks he took a deep breath and launched into a fanfare-type melody by doubling the notes with both hands an octave apart. Thus he announced a new composition called "Sometime Ago," which soon would become one of the most popular repertoire tunes of his new group, Return to Forever. He seemed to engage in a free conversation between segments of unison melodies and short harmonic interludes for close to three minutes. After the second interlude the unison melodies are played two octaves apart for a larger sound effect. The A-minor key provides the framework for moving easily up and down on the white keys. At 2:42 we hear a descending cascade of triads before he launches into a Latin-tinged rhythm pattern at 2:50 and everyone's toes start moving along. With a steady groove, Corea repeatedly leaves the white-key tonality as if he were exploring the sound before settling back into the A-minor grooves. At 3:50 we hear the swaying melody that becomes a repeating theme and would later be matched with the words "Oh, the music, it was playing—oh, the firelight, it was dancing." Manfred Eicher and the studio engineers are certainly dancing now; the cold April day seems to transform into a warm summer evening with laughter in the air. There it is again at 4:16; the melody ascends crystal clear followed by two-handed rhythms bringing out the percussive qualities of the piano.

Everyone is in a trancelike state moving to the rhythmic minor sounds, but suddenly—at 5:03—Corea transforms the scenery with a complete switch to A major. This new happy melody will later be matched with the words "Sometime ago I had a dream—it was happy, it was lasting, it was free." At 5:22 we're back into the minor sounds of the chorus. As if to remind us that we just heard the main verse and chorus of the composition, Corea plays it again, switching to the second verse at 5:51 followed by another chorus. At 6:30 the party gets wild with harmonic side steps on the black keys and stabbing fifth interval accents in the left hand. After a final downward spiral in triplets the dancers disband and by 7:20 the rhythm is free with sporadic hints of the original melody; the dream slowly dissolves and we're back into reality spiraling down the natural A-minor scale to a final octave in the bass and right-hand sprinkles.

Sometime ago I had a dream—it was happy, it was lasting, it was free—

LET'S TAKE A LISTEN TO "SPAIN"

From *Light as a Feather* by Return to Forever, Polydor 827 148-2, February 1973, recorded October 8 and 15, 1972, at I.B.C. Sound Recording Studios, London, England, featuring Flora Purim (vocals), Joe Farrell (saxophone/flute), Chick Corea (piano), Stanley Clarke (bass), Airto Moreira (drums, percussion)

Only eight months after recording their debut album and two months after the birth of Purim's and Moreira's daughter Diana, Return to Forever is back in the studio, this time in London with a new contract by major label Polydor. Even though Manfred Eicher at ECM has been supportive of the new sound and music, the debut album was only released in Europe and American distribution is minimal at this point. Audiences are reacting enthusiastically to the new sound and Polydor is one of the leaders in the American market. The group is excited about the industry support and the new material has been well rehearsed. Next on the recording plan is Corea's song "Spain." Corea was in love with Miles Davis's *Sketches of Spain*[11] album, arranged by Gil Evans. Especially Evans's treatment of the second movement of Joaquin Rodrigo's *Concierto de Aranjuez* had fascinated him and he played around with the theme, extended it, and added some additional melodies. Earlier in 1972 Corea had written out and arranged four of these melodic variations into a piece he titled "Spain."

Corea sits down at the Fender Rhodes piano and starts playing Rodrigo's beginning of the adagio movement, accompanying the original melody with colorful harmonies, while Moreira empties the rainmaker and Clarke bows long notes on the bass. As he holds the last chord he looks up and with a quick nod dictates the fast tempo going into the first of his melodic variations. Everyone is ready for the tricky hits after this first unison line; after all, the group has been playing this repertoire for several months now on the road as Stan Getz. Moreira sets them up on the drums and Farrell's flute soars on top. Moreira settles into a flamenco-inspired groove and Purim vocalizes along to the second melody variation. For the third melody variation played in unison at 1:32, everyone who has their hands free starts clapping along. The joy and excitement fill the room, enticing many future audiences and listeners to drop everything and join the party. One more time—just like in the original concerto, we'll get to hear the whole section including the clapping with some added cheers and hollers a second time.

At 2:10 we're in the main chorus section, the part that will provide the vehicle for the solo improvisations and that features melodic variation four. Clarke now settles into a samba pattern on the bass matching Moreira's drum groove. Purim's wordless vocals weave seamless echoes around the flute melody. Similar to the classical rondo form, melodic variations two and three are revisited one more time, setting the stage for the flute solo. At 2:46 Farrell takes off, soaring high over the samba rhythms provided by drums, bass, and keyboard. By the fourth chorus the excitement is building and Corea spices up the texture with some salsa patterns. One more chorus and Farrell cues the band to return to the previous ritornello interlude at 4:33. Now it's Corea's turn to dig deep into the keys of the Fender Rhodes and display his virtuosity. By the third chorus he reaches higher and higher on the keyboard, extending the harmonic structures, and reaches the climax by the fifth chorus before returning to the ritornello at 6:57. The dynamics get soft this time at 7:35 to provide Clarke the opportunity to develop his bass solo. His fingers move at lightning speed up and down the strings supported with echoes and rhythmic ideas from the keyboard. One last ritornello at 8:38 and we're back to the beginning of the song at 9:05. With loud cheers the band enters the final clapping unison section and races to a successful end with three final chord flourishes and added chorus effect on the keyboard. As the sound fades away they look at each other and nod in agreement—after three hours this is the take, and it clocks in at nearly ten minutes! For generations to come, this recording becomes a symbol of pure fun music making based on beautiful melodies and virtuosic improvisations. And, of course, upon release of the album *Light as a Feather* in 1973, this specific recording garnered Grammy nominations for Best Instrumental Arrangement and Best Instrumental Jazz Performance by a Group.

Having a "hit" can be a blessing and a curse—audiences will expect to hear the same song over and over and the artist will face the challenge of keeping it fresh. Corea describes the process in a 2011 interview for the *Atlantic*: "By 1976 or so, I started to tire of the song. I started playing really perverted versions of it—I'd refer to it just for a second, then I'd go off on an improvisation. Once the acoustic band was in action, sometime around '85, I decided to try my hand at a rearrangement of the piece. Then there was the orchestral arrangement. Even with my current band, Return to Forever IV, we're still playing 'Spain.' We've gone back to the original arrangement."[12]

5

RETURN TO FOREVER—ELECTRIC

The second incarnation of Return to Forever with Bill Connors on electric guitar, Stanley Clarke on bass, and Lenny White on drums revealed their electric sound with the 1973 release of *Hymn of the Seventh Galaxy*[1] on the Polydor label. The compositions depart from traditional song forms with extended groove elements and solo sections as well as heavy use of electronic instruments and effects. Initially drummer Steve Gadd joined the studio recordings at New York's Record Plant Studios in August 1973. But when it became clear that he would not be able to tour with the band, the repertoire was rerecorded with Lenny White on drums; the original tracks with Steve Gadd were never released. *Hymn of the Seventh Galaxy* is widely regarded as a milestone in the development of the jazz-rock genre. The fusion of genres on this specific recording actually includes elements of Latin jazz, psychedelic rock, and funk, as well as avant-garde. The *AllMusic* review of the album celebrates the quality of the compositions that make the recording an "indispensable disc of '70s Fusion."[2]

The inspiration for composing with a string of themes rather than the traditional song format was rooted in Corea's work with Miles Davis's groups and especially the recording of *Bitches Brew*. In a 1975 interview for *Jazz Forum* about the creation of *Hymn of the Seventh Galaxy* he explains:

> I remember when I was working with Miles Davis, one way that he used to put his music together was that he would go from theme to theme. He would play a theme, then we would make something with

that, and when he felt that there was no more for that, he'd play another theme and we'd make something with that. There was one point where I liked the performance part of doing that without stopping. I liked to go from theme to theme. And then that made me look at classical form structure, too, in which there are various movements to a piece of music like a suite. And then I also came to experiment with that idea, with circles too, where we would use various themes for a piece.[3]

The initial Return to Forever principle of finding ways to communicate with the audience was a guiding factor for including the lead voice of the electric guitar and increased experimentation with electronic keyboards and synthesizers. Other groups were experimenting with similar new methods of communication, and Corea's former *Bitches Brew* bandmate, guitarist John McLaughlin, became increasingly successful with his groundbreaking Mahavishnu Orchestra. The group included of course McLaughlin's lightning-fast guitar improvisations, also electric violin leads, and a unique fusion of Indian ragas and rhythms with jazz and rock. In the 1972 *DownBeat* Readers Poll, the Mahavishnu Orchestra had an unprecedented sweep of all major awards. The group won Jazz Album of the Year, Pop Album of the Year, and Rock, Pop and Blues Group of the Year for their second recording, *The Inner Mounting Flame*.[4] When John McLaughlin re-formed the Mahavishnu Orchestra in 1973, the same year Return to Forever went electric, he asked Corea for recommendations for a keyboard player who could also sing. Corea recommended Gayle Moran after he had heard her sing in *Jesus Christ Superstar* and made her acquaintance. Audiences tended to compare the groups for their sound and approach at the time, and Corea tried to break away from such comparisons (and it should also be noted that Moran became a member of Return to Forever as Gayle Moran Corea by the 1977 recording of *Musicmagic*):[5]

Well, I became intrigued with the modern way of playing electric guitar, the sound of the guitar and also what a familiar language it creates in the world: the lead guitar player. And it seems like a very modern instrument of communication. In the same way thinking the Steinway piano is a very beautiful instrument but is not so much a modern instrument of communication. It's more the electric piano and the synthesizer which are conducive to the kind of performances and the kind of sound language that is now becoming familiar. So I

> thought I'd like that, I would like to take a very, very familiar common form of music, rhythm section, electric bass, drums, electric piano, lead guitar, and then write my own music in my own way for it, so that there would be no barrier between an audience and the feeling of the music, and so they could relate immediately. I think this was a very, very successful action because people, now that we've been playing for a year, don't say any more how we sound like John McLaughlin. Now they begin to be interested in the actual music we play.[6]

With the initial momentum in popularity for Return to Forever due to the success of *Light as a Feather*,[7] the new album had to be released quickly and tours were lined up. The band was in the studio just a few months after finding Bill Connors and the music had only been played in a few initial rehearsals. Corea recalls the urgency of creating new music for the band: "For instance in this particular period with the *Hymn Of The Seventh Galaxy*[8]—music, I had a very quick task to do. I had a tour to make and a new band to put together. So I very quickly wrote music, brrr . . . And we rehearsed two days, three hours each, and I wrote the parts out for everybody."[9]

The new electric sound was received with enthusiasm by jazz audiences and rock fans alike. Over the next three years Return to Forever became one of the most successful groups of the decade. "We played as loud if not louder than rock bands," recalls Clarke, "and the audiences were different. Guys would come up to you and thank us for turning them on to Miles or Coltrane, but it was against the likes of Yes and ELP that the band was compared."[10] Soon the group outgrew their original performance venues such as the Village Vanguard in Manhattan and attracted audiences of three thousand plus in concert halls worldwide. Corea acknowledges: "Our audience has changed vastly. Maybe it's not so much changed as expanded. I don't feel we've lost too many old fans. We have lost some jazz fans at a rough guess maybe about 20% of the people who liked my earlier records and the first version of Return to Forever. We're not commercial in their eyes. But we've retained 80% of them and we've reached a whole new group of people, especially the young rock audience."[11]

The group was well aware of the change in audience demographics; but the aspirations were not rock superstardom but rather the ability to inspire listeners on a high aesthetic level. The compositional aspect of the group was a key ingredient to its success. Clarke recalls:

> "Out of the three top fusion bands—Mahavishnu Orchestra, Weather Report and Return to Forever—we had the best compositions. We used to do lots of gigs with Fleetwood Mac, Bachman Turner Overdrive, David Bowie. We used to blow those bands off the stage because people would hear all this stuff that they'd never heard. It was intricate music. We were precise, much like classical music, and audiences had never seen that. When that door was opened we walked right through it."[12]

A recurring theme in interviews with Chick Corea is his quest to communicate with audiences on a deep and honest level without compromising the essence of the music.

> "Another reward that I'm seeking to get is firm acceptance of the idea that it's not necessary to be dishonest in order to communicate, that you can really be yourself and still communicate to everybody without compromising your own true goals and your own creative reality. I want to get agreement on that idea because I know it's true. So the way I can get agreement on it, is by us doing it."[13]

Corea admits, though, that technical virtuosity can sometimes be a hurdle to simple communication, and some critics compared the group's performances to technical thunderstorms.[14] He takes his inspiration for connecting with the audience from the likes of Sly Stone and Stevie Wonder but repeatedly confirms that he would never intentionally "water down" the essence of his music in order to reach wider audiences.

After just a few months of touring, Bill Connors decided to quit the band and pursue a solo acoustic career. He subsequently recorded three albums with ECM but disappeared quickly from the international touring scene. In a 2005 interview he regretfully mentioned: "Maybe I should've just taken a few days off. It was a little rash."[15] Personality conflicts and leadership style seemed to be the main issues. Connors told *Guitar* magazine over a decade after he'd left that "Chick had a lot of ideas that were part of his involvement with Scientology. I wasn't allowed to control my own solos. Then we'd receive written notes about what clothes we could wear, and graphic charts where we had to rate ourselves every night, eventually I just felt screwed around. In the end my only power was to quit."[16]

Al Di Meola, a nineteen-year-old guitarist from Bergenfield, New Jersey, who just started at Berklee College of Music, seemed to have the right mix of skills to replace Bill Connors. He played electric guitar with a jazz background and he could read music. In fact, his fellow local guitarists ostracized him for not fitting in with his jazz-rock leanings. While the common rock language at the time included playing riffs and pentatonics, Di Meola was trained to play scales using the jazz language by his teacher Bob Aslanian. Stanley Clarke describes him as a "blank canvas" who could play and read the parts and was brave enough to play his first concert at Carnegie Hall straight after Billy Connors had left, with a band that Clarke describes as "tight and ferocious like a lion."[17] Di Meola recalls in a 2003 interview with Anil Prasad:

> It was a dream come true. It was my favorite group. Chick was my favorite writer. I was in probably the greatest group for an electric guitar player possible. Chick was writing the most incredible music for electric guitar. And I was in the forefront. I was the guy who got the hippest guitar parts on the planet Earth at the time. It's really true. I'm not bragging. Mahavishnu was not a compositional band. Go back and listen to their records—all they were doing was blowing. It was just tons of improvising and playing at fast tempos. But RTF was a composition band, way more than Mahavishnu and Weather Report. It was really classical rock and jazz, with tons of structure and parts, and the guitar in the forefront. It was great and really challenging. I took it very seriously.[18]

Di Meola's tenure with Return to Forever includes the recordings *Where Have I Known You Before* (Polydor, 1974),[19] *No Mystery* (Polydor, 1975),[20] and *Romantic Warrior* (Columbia, 1976)[21] during the time when the group enjoyed its highest commercial success. Over those three years, this specific quartet was able to develop its complex, virtuosic playing style with a focus on extended and refined compositions to unprecedented heights. In fact, *No Mystery* earned a Grammy Award for Best Jazz Instrumental Performance and *Romantic Warrior* became Corea's highest-selling recording with more than five hundred thousand copies to date. Di Meola's guitar pyrotechnics are a trademark of the group, overshadowing Connors's early contributions: "I don't have a huge ego, but it still hurt when people would tell me that I must've listened to a lot of Al Di Meola (who replaced Connors in Return to Forever)," Connors said. "I was robbed of my identity, that my guitar was like a credit card that had been stolen and I'd been left to pay the bill."[22]

With a new recording contract from Columbia Records, a Grammy Award, and the extraordinary commercial success of *Romantic Warrior*, the news of Corea's decision to break up the group came as a shock and surprise in 1976. Speculations for the split included artistic differences, ego clashes, and possibly Clarke's decision to leave Scientology. Each group member also had solo projects at that point, and the various activities interfered with the band's focus and leadership. Clarke compares it to the dynamics in Art Blakey's various groups, where outstanding band members often were discovered by record labels and ended up starting solo careers. He recalls: "Nat Weiss was sitting in the audience and he said, 'You have a lot of charisma, do you want to make a record?' I said yes: Next thing I know I'm up in his office working on a solo record for Nemperor, which was connected to Atlantic, which could sell records a lot better [than Polydor]. Then my records started competing with the band, and Al and Lenny started making records. Chick woke up one day and said, 'How are we going to organize all this stuff?'"[23] Lenny White confirmed the unique situation and pointed out that for the first time in music industry history all members of a group with a major label recording contract (Columbia) simultaneously held contracts with other labels. It was a situation actually encouraged by management at the time with the intention to nurture everyone's own self-expression and projects.[24]

Corea's creativity was flying high, though, and a new album under his own name, *The Leprechaun*,[25] was ready for release in 1976 (Polydor) and earned two more Grammy Awards for Best Instrumental Jazz Performance and Best Instrumental Arrangement for "The Leprechaun's Dream, Pt. 1." The personnel for this recording included fifteen musicians, including the ethereal vocals of his new wife, Gayle Moran Corea, and a string quartet.

The seventh and final studio album of the group Return to Forever titled *Musicmagic* (Columbia, 1977)[26] included only Corea and bassist Stanley Clarke as returning members. Rounding out the group were Gerry Brown on drums, Joe Farrell on saxophone and flute, Gayle

Moran Corea on vocals and keys, and a brass quartet. The group recorded a two-LP live set on May 20 and 21 at the Palladium in New York City during the supporting tour for *Musicmagic*, which ended up being the last recording under the Return to Forever name until the reunion tour in 2012. Another perk of this tour was also a meeting with President Jimmy Carter in June 1977. Columbia Records released a *Best of Return to Forever*[27] collection in 1980 that did not contain any new materials but a collection of tracks owned by the label.

Corea's creativity was running on overdrive from 1976 to 1980, producing six studio albums with large ensembles as well as two duet albums with vibraphonist Gary Burton, two duet albums with fellow pianist Herbie Hancock, and one acoustic jazz quartet release with Joe Henderson, Roy Haynes, and Gary Peacock in addition to the final Return to Forever compilations. That's a total of fourteen releases in five years. Even when considering that five of these recordings are live sets, the sheer amount and diversity documents Corea's quest for exploring new creative outlets in intimate acoustic settings while pushing the envelope of the popular jazz fusion genre with extended compositions, large ensembles, electronic sounds, and displays of virtuosity at the end of his second career decade. We'll close out this chapter discussing the six large ensemble releases *The Leprechaun*,[28] *My Spanish Heart*,[29] *The Mad Hatter*,[30] *Friends*,[31] *Secret Agent*,[32] and *Tap Step*.[33] The unique dynamics of playing duets and Corea's various duet partners will be the topic of the next chapter.

The Leprechaun features a complete string and brass section and was released in 1976 on the Polydor label. It reached No. 1 on the Billboard Jazz charts and won Corea two more Grammy Awards for Best Instrumental Jazz Performance, Individual or Group for the album and for Best Instrumental Arrangement Grammy Award for "Leprechaun's Dream, Pt. 1." Images and ideas about the Leprechaun character provide the musical titles. The eclectic styles ranging from ragtime influences to funk are in contrast to the studio album *My Spanish Heart*, released the same year as a double LP and featuring a strong return to Corea's Latin roots and now one of his trademark albums. *DownBeat* magazine awarded a rare five-star review for the compositional masterpiece featuring strings and brass galore as well as plenty of electronic sounds and Gayle Moran Corea's ethereal vocals. In his *All-Music* review, Thom Jurek praises the depth of *My Spanish Heart*:

"Simply put, he [Corea] was compositionally and intellectually at the top of his game, and this record, despite the many of his that haven't aged well, still surprises despite its production shortcomings."[34] Even with the Spanish reference and a return to Latin American rhythms it is clear at this point that Corea's compositional style is far more complex and eclectic than any stylistic labels available. In a study exploring the jazz-flamenco connections, Juan Zagalaz notes: "What Corea does show is a clear tendency towards experimentation and stylistic openness, integrating basic elements of jazz with modern synthesizers, string sections and vocal ensembles, and Latin sounds transcending those of the distant Spain of de Falla and Rodrigo, all while creating music that always sounds like his own."[35]

When Corea opened up an advance copy of the December 1977 *DownBeat* magazine featuring the annual Readers Poll, he found his name listed twelve times in eleven different categories. He placed first in the Composer division. He also topped the list in the Electric Piano category. Return to Forever placed second (to Weather Report) for the Jazz Group awards, and RTF also placed in the unlikely category of Rock/Blues Group. Two albums—*My Spanish Heart* and *Musicmagic*—appeared in the Jazz Album of the Year listings. Corea's name appeared in six other categories as well: Synthesizer, Acoustic Piano, Hall of Fame, Jazz Man of the Year, Arranger, and Rock/Blues Musician. Lee Underwood, a writer for *DownBeat* magazine, had brought the copy along to an interview about the upcoming album *The Mad Hatter*. Corea smiled at the amount and eclectic mix of his nominations: "I don't feel stuck in any one style of music," he said. "My attitude is real open, and I like to have fun with all of the different kinds of music. I like to compose in various ways; I like to improvise. I like electric instruments; I like acoustic instruments. I love it all, so that's how it comes out."[36]

The Mad Hatter was Corea's first concept album where the music is composed based on various characters in the popular children's story *Alice in Wonderland*. Of course there is the Mad Hatter and also Alice as well as Tweedle Dee and Tweedle Dum. The compositions are heavily influenced by the music of Bela Bartok, a Hungarian composer of the early twentieth century deeply rooted in folk music traditions. Corea explains: "I bought the early works on record, and I bought some of his [Bartok's] music. I listened and grooved on his music, which I love, and I read a book on the last five years of his life, and just got into him. I've always liked him, but this time something happened. Beyond just listening and enjoying, I hit the level where I really began to understand fully what the guy is all about and what he's doing, above and beyond the notes. Then, at the level right above that, I got it. That's what he's all about."[37]

Most composers would take a year to write an album's worth of music at the level of complexity recorded on *The Mad Hatter*. For Corea it was a three-week process to complete all music and arrangements. Here is a glimpse into Corea's compositional process and work habits:

> I took a week of what I call research. I listened to music. I played and improvised. I taped some stuff. I hung out and looked at the night sky. You know—like "being an artist." The next two weeks, I sat down with my scores and wrote it.
>
> When I compose for a record, I work 18–20 hours a day. I eat and sleep very little and I feel fantastically good! I have my business people leave, and I don't take phone calls or have visitors. I isolate myself, and get that creative flow going. Once it starts, it's like a snowball, you know? It's not frantic at all, but relaxed. When I finally sit down with my score I'm there with it for a lot of hours.
>
> I don't drink anything, nor do I take any drugs at all, not even aspirin. I gave up those ways of getting high about ten years ago. Drugs are poisons. My mind works at its best and clearest when I don't put poisons in my body. You can take any poison, just enough to get your body a little crazy, and it creates effects. People love these effects, but in reality they actually numb a person.[38]

In 1978, Polydor released two more studio albums, *Friends* and *Secret Agent*, after the March release of *The Mad Hatter*, as well as two live albums, *An Evening with Herbie Hancock & Chick Corea*[39] and *Return to Forever—Live*.[40] The album covers of *Friends* featured a group of Smurfs performing music together. It's a return to the acoustic quartet sound and received a Grammy at the 1979 Awards for Best Jazz Instrumental Performance, Group. Besides Corea on piano and keyboards, the "friends" featured are Joe Farrell on saxophones and flute, Eddie Gomez on bass, and Steve Gadd on drums. *Friends* featured more intricate group improvisations rather than compositional depth as in the previous albums and the results are some fine musical moments rewarded by another Grammy.

In contrast, *Secret Agent* is an independent collection of eight Corea compositions and one by Hungarian composer Bela Bartok with ensembles ranging from two to twelve pieces. The Polydor release capped off 1978 as an "almost impossibly active"[41] year with three studio albums and two live releases. The personnel was loosely based on the final *Return to Forever* incarnation with a horn and a string section on many tracks. In addition to several vocal tracks by Gayle Moran, Al Jarreau gets a guest spot on the song "Hot News Blues." In his AllAboutJazz.com review, John Kelman points out that "Corea's eclectic aesthetic leaves few stylistic stones unturned."[42] The album cover displays Corea in a trench coat and hat, posing mysteriously in a shadowy environment—an image of the unpredictability of his creative outbursts, musical explorations, and things to come.

The final album in the large ensemble series, *Tap Step*,[43] was released on the Warner label in 1980 to mixed reviews. The album features Corea in uniform beating the bass drum certainly indicating his leadership of the group. It features a host of artists, reuniting with initial Return to Forever partners Flora Purim and Airto Moreira as well as other friends including Allen Vizzutti, Bunny Brunel, Don Alias, Gayle Moran Corea, Hubert Laws, Jamie Faunt, Joe Farrell, Joe Henderson, Laudir DeOliveira, Nain Brunel, Shelby Flint, Stanley Clarke, and Tom Brechtlein. Similarly it features a host of musical styles from Brazilian Samba to funk grooves and a nod to Charlie Parker with the title tune "Tap Step." Bunny Brunel's fretless bass as well as the sound of the Rhodes and the Moog synthesizer lead the sound of the compilation. With only three weeks on the Billboard charts and a peak position of 170, its commercial success was mediocre. With a three-star review in *DownBeat* magazine, the close mix of style and cliché becomes a point of criticism with, of course, acknowledgment of the ever-present high quality of artistry.[44]

The variety of collaborations and new groups over the next three decades can also be described as "impossibly active." An attempt for a Return to Forever reunion in 1983 only resulted in a short tour, but three decades after the impossibly active year, in 2008, the nucleus with Stanley Clarke, Al Di Meola, and Larry White reunited for the release of *Return to Forever Returns*[45] and a highly anticipated world tour.

Together with other icons of the jazz fusion era who initially set out as members of Miles Davis's *Bitches Brew* group, such as John McLaughlin, who founded the Mahavishnu Orchestra; Herbie Hancock, leader of the Headhunters; and Joe Zawinul of Weather Report legacy, Return to Forever facilitated the marriage of jazz with the evolving global pop and rock styles. The world fusion movement of the nineties brought about further styles categorized as klezmer jazz, Latin jazz, M-Base jazz, New Orleans jazz, acid jazz, electronica, Eastern European jazz, and so on.[46] There was a sense of exploration, collaboration, and globalization that carried the art form into the new millennium. New and exciting forms of stylistic collaborations constantly arise from explorations in small clubs, the support of specialty labels and jazz organizations, and global connections facilitated by new technology.

In closing, here are a few quotes and thoughts on the impact of Chick Corea's willingness to explore new grounds and his prolific output during the seventies that set the standards for performance practice, quality, and style for decades to come:

> I had always observed that the better the music was, the better the response was. This was completely opposite to what I was being told. So, I thought, that thing of playing down to audiences is a real result of some kind of disrespect for one another or some kind of other motivation besides art. And I thought, "I don't agree with that. I'm going to put a band together and not play down to audiences, but make the quality of the music as high as I possibly can." And it works—in my life it has always worked. I found that the better I play—the more feeling and time I devote to my music, the higher the quality is at the concerts that I perform—the better the people like it.[47]

When interviewer Mike Haid asked Corea, "Can't we look at the Seventies fusion movement as an electric bebop era?" he responded:

> Right, and the whole signal to me is that we're not living life to the fullest if we get stuck in the past, and say, "That was the greatest" and "It's not happening now," and send our statement there. In order to give life to your statement, you have to now say, "Okay, it's not happening now, so therefore I'm going to create something to make it happen now. I'm gonna do something about it. I'm gonna open up a club or I'm gonna take it upon myself to create a new form of music

> and pursue my dream as a musician, because I want to revive that spirit."[48]

And drummer Lenny White summed up Corea's artistic spirit very well: "I have to address the mindset that Chick Corea has. He has always been true to what he wants to present and put across, even to the point where he just doesn't make compromises. And there is a part of me that respects that a great deal and we need people like that within the artistic community to help bolster the true meaning of an artist and the artist's position in society."[49]

LET'S TAKE A LISTEN TO "DUEL OF THE JESTER AND THE TYRANT"

From *Romantic Warrior* by Return to Forever, Columbia CK-46109, 1976, recorded at Caribou Ranch, Colorado, February 1976, with Chick Corea (keyboards), Al Di Meola (guitar), Stanley Clarke (bass), Lenny White (drums)

Romantic Warrior was the biggest commercial success for the group Return to Forever as it was eventually gold certified, peaking at No. 35 on the Billboard 200 in 1976, and No. 3 on the Jazz Album charts. It was also the final recording of the quartet with Al Di Meola on guitar—often hailed as one of the most influential and powerful jazz fusion collaborations. After winning their first Grammy Award for the *No Mystery* album and touring around the world for the past three years, the group was at the top of its game and excited to record the first album for one of the most prestigious record labels in the world, Columbia Records. In February of 1976 the group headed to a new studio, the isolated Caribou Ranch in a remote part of Colorado. Progressive rock groups such as Yes were filling stadiums, and keyboardist Rick Wakeman had recently released some solo projects with medieval themes. Corea was very impressed with Wakeman's work and liked the image of medieval heroes and warriors as an expression of the powerful musicianship and new exploration of territory. The goal of this recording was to reach the progressive rock audiences and attain the highest levels of musicality.

The last tune for today's session is a Corea composition titled "Duel of the Jester and the Tyrant." This is quite an extended composition with many different sections and texture changes. It feels more like a soundtrack to a film or an electronic symphony than a jazz tune. This will take a lot of concentration, and in order to get all the transitions and sound adjustments right, everyone lines up several music stands to spread out the long scores and checks their equipment settings. The sound engineer gives a thumbs-up and Corea starts with a low sounding, atonal and somewhat disconnected sequence of organ notes. The drums enter with rolls and accents and Corea holds chords with his left hand on the synthesizer while playing melodies on the Moog keyboard that sound like the announcement of the Jester and the Tyrant ready to engage in their duel: may the games begin. Suspension builds as the synthesizer chords fade into single tremolo notes and bass and guitar enter. The melody instruments play in unison and with a series of chromatic chords on the Fender Rhodes, Corea sets up the first theme. At 1:33 the harmonies settle into a repeating sequence of four chords, and a happy motive on the Fender Rhodes keyboard gets the listener hooked. It's time for Di Meola to take the first guitar solo. He immediately displays his virtuosic capabilities, but it's not time yet for takeoff. The music settles back into the initial melody at 3:20 and the introductory chord sequence for another minute before Corea moves back to the Moog synthesizer and begins soloing. The excitement builds and he bends the notes with the joystick in expressive guitar-like outbursts. At 6:00 we return to the initial unison line.

It seems that the Jester and the Tyrant now enter a new stage in their duel as the music starts swinging and the bass introduces a funky groove supported by a clavinet sequence. At 7:12 Di Meola provides another glimpse into his technical capabilities, but a comical ARP synthesizer sequence keeps interrupting him and makes everyone almost laugh with its humorous sound setting. It seems that the Jester is leading the battle and showcasing funny gimmicks for the audience. At 8:52 a powerful drum break sets an end to the antics and leads us to a new announcement sequence similar to the initial fanfare. Is this the end of the duel? Corea moves to the clavinet and plays a polyphonic, classical-sounding solo interlude reminiscent of a Bach piece. The initial announcement theme is played in a question-and-response manner with guitar lead until the whole band settles into a final and complex unison theme announcing the end of the duel. Di Meola sure displayed his assertive guitar playing that had earned him Corea's compliments when he first joined the group: "You know, I really like the fact that you play with conviction, even if you make a mistake. I like that, too. When you make a mistake, it's really out there—boom. I don't like guys who are afraid, and everything they play sounds afraid."[50] It seems that neither the Jester nor the Tyrant won, but the battle sure was entertaining and exciting for the audience members to witness.

Here is the complete synthesizer orchestration used on the recording:[51]

0:00–0:15	Minimoog, Yamaha organ
0:15–0:50	ARP Odyssey, Polymoog
0:50–1:10	Yamaha organ
1:10–1:18	Minimoog
1:18–1:32	Fender Rhodes
1:32–2:30	Oberheim Eight Voice (string pad), Rhodes, Minimoog
2:30–3:20	Rhodes
3:20–4:48	Alternating Rhodes and Minimoog solos, Oberheim Eight Voice
4:48–5:58	Minimoog solo, Rhodes
5:58–6:18	Rhodes, Minimoog
6:18–6:49	Minimoog, Rhodes, Clavinet
6:49–7:12	Clavinet
7:12–7:38	Clavinet
7:38–8:00	Polymoog (high stabs), Clavinet
8:00–8:22	Clavinet
8:22–8:46	Polymoog (high stabs), Clavinet
8:46–9:12	Clavinet
9:12–9:18	Minimoog
9:18–9:35	Yamaha organ
9:35–9:55	Polymoog, ARP Odyssey
9:55–10:23	Polymoog (bass), Minimoog (lead)

10:23–10:34	Yamaha organ (plucky sound), Minimoog read
10:34–10:55	Yamaha organ (plucky sound), ARP Odyssey (sustained sound)
10:55–11:04	Minimoog lead
11:04–end	Yamaha organ (pads), ARP Odyssey (horn-like part), Minimoog lead

6

PLAYING WITH FRIENDS

One of the most intimate and rewarding, but also challenging, settings in jazz is playing duets. It demands a high level of interaction, listening, virtuosity, and personality match from the performers in order to be meaningful and rewarding. Chick Corea has engaged in the art of the duet since his release *Crystal Silence* (ECM) with longtime duet partner Gary Burton in 1972. Other duet partners include fellow pianists Herbie Hancock, Friedrich Gulda, Hiromi, Gonzalo Rubalcaba, and Stefano Bollani, as well as vocalist Bobby McFerrin, banjoist Bela Fleck, and many more. Gary Burton explained in an interview about their thirty-five-year relationship that garnered them six shared Grammy Awards: "The duo format offers a unique method of musical communication. If you're playing alone, it's like you're giving a speech. And if you're in a group, you are part of a good discussion, with lots of lively side conversations going on. But if you are in a duo, it's like having an intimate conversation with one of your best friends. You finish each other's sentences; you can tell what the other person is thinking; you know when to speak and when to listen."[1]

At the end of a 1971 concert at the Munich Jazz Festival that featured various solo acts, Chick Corea and Gary Burton found themselves behind the stage as the only two volunteers for an encore jam when the enthusiastic audience was clapping for more. Corea remembers: "The German audience loved the show, so they were like hootin' and hollerin' at the end of the show, and we were standing backstage, and the promoter was going, 'Why don't you guys go out there and play an encore.' So I was standing next to Gary, and his vibes were out on the stage, and I thought, 'Gee, "La Fiesta" is a pretty simple tune, it has one chord in it—you want to go out and play?' So we improvised 'La Fiesta.' Manfred Eicher heard it and invited us to do a duet."[2]

The result was the 1973 release *Crystal Silence*[3] featuring a set of Corea and Burton originals as well as Michael Gibbs's "Feelings and Things" and Steve Swallow's "Arise, Her Eyes." Of the three days allotted for rehearsal and recording, the duo only took three hours to complete the album[4] with single takes on all tunes, except two takes on "Senor Mouse." The nine-minute title track, "Crystal Silence," is a timeless piece of beauty and depth where the two come together for a singular soundscape. The listening example at the end of this chapter includes a detailed analysis of the piece.

The partnership of Burton and Corea continues after more than forty years of multiple tours and seven duet albums with six shared Grammy Awards. Burton describes their extraordinary rapport: "If I were to rate it on a 1 to 10 scale, I would say most of the musicians I have played with are a six or a seven. With Chick, it has always been a 10. And it was that way immediately."[5] Here is the discography of their collaborative recordings:

Crystal Silence (ECM 1973)[6]
Duet (ECM 1979)[7]
In Concert, Zurich, October 28, 1979 (ECM 1980)[8]
Native Sense: The New Duets (Concord 1997)[9]
Like Minds (Concord 1998)[10]
The New Crystal Silence—Double Live CD (Concord 2008)[11]
Hot House (Concord 2012)[12]

Guitarist/composer Pat Metheny contributed the liner notes to *The New Crystal Silence* and expressed his respect for the high artistry and virtuosity of the duo. He writes: "I have often contended that Gary Burton is one of the best improvisers of all time—not just as a vibist, but among all players. The range of melodic options that he brings to the table nightly is staggering in its vastness. One of the great features of this collaboration is the perfect fit that this format offers Gary. Playing with Chick affords him the chance to investigate the full range of his gifts in this area completely."

A special attraction of this specific duo is the unique combination of timbre with the bell-like sound of the vibraphone and the piano both playing melodies and harmonies as well as their obvious pure joy of creating music together. Corea continued to engage in a wide range of duo projects over the years, several with other pianists. His motivation to continuously seek out new project challenges provides the various scenarios that might evolve and differ from project to project, from performance to performance. A collaboration is similar to a movie script with the creation of a recorded soundtrack, various live performances, and a basic message—but in contrast to a movie, collaborative projects change from event to event and include a chance factor similar to a game. The challenge of playing the game becomes the attraction of the new project.[13]

Herbie Hancock, whom Corea had traded places with in Blue Mitchell's group as well as sharing keyboard duties in Miles Davis's *In a Silent Way* and *Bitches Brew* sessions, became his first piano duet partner. Extensive touring resulted in the 1978 double LP compilation *An Evening with Herbie Hancock and Chick Corea: In Concert* (Columbia/Legacy 1978). The four LP sides feature extended versions of the Disney classic "Someday My Prince Will Come," a striding version of Gershwin's "Liza" as well as Hancock's "Maiden Voyage" and "February Moment," a collaborative tune titled "Button Up," and a twenty-two-minute version of Corea's "La Fiesta." In contrast to the initial studio recordings with Gary Burton, the music was selected from live recordings at the Masonic Auditorium in San Francisco, the Dorothy Chandler Pavilion in Los Angeles, Golden Hall in San Diego, and the Hill Auditorium in Ann Arbor.

Each pianist appears on a different channel on the recording in order to create a live concert effect. The two masters draw from every aspect of the pianistic palette as melodies soar, harmonic flourishes are exchanged, marching bass lines guide the rhythmic proceedings, tremolos shine, and every so often the strings inside the piano get plucked and pulled. Corea remembers: "The record with Herbie was . . . gee, just another great musical experience in my life. Hooking up with Herbie who was just one of my heroes, and being able to spend that much time with him playing piano duets on the road was kind of a breakthrough, actually. It was kind of strange to play a whole concert with two pianos. At first, we thought, when we were fooling around with it, we kept thinking like we were getting in each other's way. Then we both had an epiphany at the same moment about how good it all sounded, what we were doing. We became very compassionate about one another's offerings to the other, like in terms of what we were creating, and made something out of everything that we threw at one another. From there on, it just became pure fun."[14]

In 2015, the two rekindled their fun and compassion thirty-seven years after the release of the live recording with a tour of more than twenty collaborative concerts around the world. While improvising freely with extensive space for interaction, the two also performed familiar songs and melodies, frequently reaching out to the audience for sing-alongs and harmonic accompaniment. *Sydney Morning Herald* reviewer John Shand called the result "extraordinarily liquid music that will live in the memory."[15] Rather than the traditional format of switching off between soloing and accompanying, the two engage in constant interaction throughout their concerts.

After the initial recording with Herbie Hancock, Corea could be found quite frequently in duet settings with other pianists. In fact, the collaboration with classical piano star Friedrich Gulda resulted in Corea's recording of the Mozart Double Piano Concerto. At Gulda's request, the two of them performed an initial concert together on June 27, 1982, at the Munich Piano Summer Festival, subsequently released under the title *The Meeting*.[16] Gulda (1930–2000) became one of the most prominent classical pianists at an early age, traveling the world with his groundbreaking interpretations of the complete Beethoven Piano Sonatas. However, disillusioned with the rigors of the classical piano circuit, he soon pushed the boundaries by adding improvisatory segments to his concerts, tapping his foot while playing Mozart in his hometown Vienna's Musikverein, and even appearing naked onstage with his girlfriend for a rendition of Schumann songs on recorder. Gulda was fascinated by jazz and a highly accomplished improviser, but jazz fans denied him a second career as a jazz pianist due to his deep roots in the classical genre. Nevertheless he kept exploring jazz through various collaborations with renowned jazz pianists such as Chick Corea, Herbie Hancock, and fellow Austrian Joe Zawinul, and after 1995 even engaged frequently into techno sessions with Liverpool DJ Vertigo.[17] At their initial concert, Gulda and Corea embarked on an exploration without a safety net. With extended improvisations on the Disney song

"Someday My Prince Will Come" and the music of Miles Davis and Johannes Brahms, they completed a journey of collaborative music making that transcends boundaries between the two players.

Corea recalled this initial concert as the inspiration for his recording of Mozart's Double Piano Concerto with the Concertgebouw Orchestra and Friedrich Gulda under the baton of Nikolaus Harnoncourt and his subsequent love affair with Mozart and classical composition. Halfway during their improvised concert, Gulda started a beautiful melody and clearly played a passage from memory while Corea paused for a minute to listen. Corea asked him about the music later and Gulda explained that he was playing a segment from a Mozart piece. Intrigued by the beauty of the music and his own limited knowledge of Mozart's music, Corea accepted Gulda's invitation to perform and record the Mozart Double Piano Concerto only six months later with the Concertgebouw Orchestra.[18] In fact, the in-depth explorations of Mozart's music resulted in a series of further performances of the concerto with fellow pianists Keith Jarrett and Makoto Ozone, as well as numerous classical compositions for various chamber music ensembles inspired by Mozart's music. Interviewed about the premiere of his *Septet for Winds, Strings, and Piano* just months after the meeting with Gulda, Corea reflected about the boundaries of musical genres: "After all, formal styles are only an afterthought—an outgrowth of the creative impulse. Nobody sits down and decides to specifically write in a predetermined style. A style is not something you learn so much as something that you synthesize. Musicians don't care if a given composition is jazz, pop, or classical music. All they care about is whether it is good music—whether it is challenging and exciting."[19]

The ongoing love affair with Mozart's music led to another Grammy-winning collaboration with fellow genre-bending vocalist Bobby McFerrin. The story seems familiar—after a concert in Stuttgart, Germany, Corea walked behind the stage with the audience clapping for more and saw vocalist Bobby McFerrin in the wings, who had been performing on the same stage the night before. Corea extended a spontaneous invitation to McFerrin to join him onstage for an encore. Corea remembers: "So he came out and we messed around heavily with 'Autumn Leaves.' It turned out to be a great, great time we had. Neither of us forgot."[20] The result was *Play*, compiled from a six-concert tour in 1990.[21] The two master improvisers explored their craft, interacted with and followed each other, and displayed their deep musical friendship in dazzling ways. Far beyond their playful interactions, the two displayed their sophisticated and genre-crossing musicianship on the 1996 release *The Mozart Sessions* on Sony Classical.[22] McFerrin conducted the Saint Paul Chamber Orchestra with Corea as the featured soloist on Mozart's Concertos for Piano and Orchestra K. 488 in A Major and K. 466 in D Minor. They successfully pushed the boundaries of the classical genre confinement with improvised introductions and unconventional cadenzas and ornamentations. After all, Mozart was known for his improvisational abilities, a talent that was seen as essential for a pianist in the eighteenth century. Contemporary critics expressed mixed opinions but admitted that the sheer joy, ability, and enthusiasm outshines any conventional requirements. Joseph Kerman contemplated in a 1997 review for *Early Music*: "Although Corea's work and that of McFerrin is not the most refined, nor 'historically aware' beyond attention to ornaments etc., in K466 their sheer musicality and passion move inexorably to fulfillment in the improvised cadenzas, which are quite marvelous in my opinion. It is harder to characterize or describe them than to say what they are not: neither Mozartian (thank heaven, this being Steinway territory) nor jazzy."[23]

Maybe the recognition of sheer musicality and passion is what draws Corea to his various duet partners. His most recent piano collaboration was with the young Japanese piano sensation Hiromi Uehara on a two-disc live compilation titled *Duet*.[24] Hiromi met Chick Corea for the first time when she was seventeen and he immediately invited her to join him at the Tokyo Blue Note. Three years later she matriculated at the Berklee College of Music in Boston where legendary pianist Ahmad Jamal became her mentor and helped produce her debut CD *Another Mind*.[25] Since then she has garnered a long list of awards for her recordings with Sonicbloom and her current trio project, even a Grammy with Stanley Clarke's group. In an interview with Larry Appelbaum, she recalls her fateful first meeting with Chick Corea:

> I met Chick for the first time when I was 17. I lived in Shizuoka and I was taking some lessons in Tokyo. That same day, Chick happened to be in the building where I was taking lessons. I got so excited and I wanted to say hello. I knocked on his door and told him: "Wow, I'm a big fan, I'm so happy to meet you in person, thank you so much for the inspiration," blah, blah. He asked me what I played. I said piano,

> and he pointed to the piano there and said, "Play something for me." So I played one of my pieces. There were two pianos there, so when I finished he began to play and we started to play together. When we finished, he asked, are you free tomorrow night? Do you want to play in my show? That was one of the craziest events of my life. I wasn't planning to spend the next day in Tokyo, so I had to book a hotel and stay over. I was only 17 and I called my mom and said, I don't know what happened but I think I'm playing with Chick Corea tomorrow night. And he called me at the end of his show and I went up and played with him. It was a completely improvised song, kind of a call and response thing. Then, ten years later, the Tokyo Jazz Festival asked me to do a duet concert with Chick. So we played together for about an hour, and this time he asked, do you want to make a record? He always surprises me.[26]

Corea extended his duet invitations to pianists around the globe with a keen sense of recognizing outstanding talent but also interactive sensibility. Cuban sensation Gonzalo Rubalcaba joined Corea during his three-week sixtieth birthday celebration at New York's legendary Blue Note featuring nine different groups. The result is a thirteen-minute tour de force of Corea's "Spain" on the 2003 release *Rendezvous in New York*.[27] A variety of piano duets were featured during Corea's eighty-engagement seventy-fifth birthday celebration at the Blue Note in New York throughout the fall of 2016. Audiences in the Italian city Orvieto got to witness the pairing of Italy's own Stefano Bollani and Chick Corea for the live recording of an acoustic piano duet concert. William Ruhlmann acknowledges the successful pairing in the AllMusic.com review of the release *Orvieto*: "And thus the veteran of Hispanic heritage and the younger Italian mix their Southern European flavors on one of the building blocks of American jazz, making for a heady musical concoction that confirms the talents of both."[28]

Many stories of these collaborations seem to have the common thread of chance meetings and impromptu performances that result in a series of concerts and recordings. Over the years, concert audiences have witnessed many more impromptu duets at events all over the world, sometimes just a guest appearance, sometimes a collaborative concert or some recordings. "The best award I get each night is after a performance and to hear the audience's appreciation of the music I've been making all these years. That's very inspiring," Corea says.[29] The most recent extended partnership actually crossed genres, generations, and musical approaches with banjo virtuoso Bela Fleck.

Initially rooted in bluegrass, Fleck soaked in the sounds of jazz growing up in New York and Boston and found his unique voice on the banjo with his group Bela Fleck and the Flecktones. The group was formed in 1988 and has garnered six Grammy Awards over the years. Chicago keyboardist/harmonica player Howard Levy was a founding member of the group but left in 1992 to spend more time with his family and less time on the road. In search for new collaborations, Fleck invited Corea to record several tracks with the group for the 1995 release *Tales from the Acoustic Planet*.[30] The two exchanged project ideas throughout their frequent encounters and finally met up in bassist Edgar Mayer's studio in Nashville, Tennessee, in 2007 for the recording of *The Enchantment*.[31] Most tracks were completed in one or two takes with extended improvisational sections, common practice for Chick Corea but a new approach for Bela Fleck: "With me, I feel like it usually takes me four of five takes to get to a level that I feel is OK to put out on a record. And the further I go, the better I usually get in a lot of areas. So Chick isn't self-conscious about his playing, and he'd always seem pretty happy with things early on. I'd be thinking, oh no, I haven't really had time to refine some of this stuff, whereas his parts already sounded refined. So we met in the middle by doing things a bit more than he's used to, and a bit less than I'm used to."[32]

Throughout 2007, the duo embarked on extensive worldwide tours and recently reunited for a series of concerts with a new repertoire. In contrast to their initial recording, the follow-up release *Two* featured a collage of highlights from their live performances, thus capturing the energy of the moment fueled by enthusiastic audiences. Despite their differences in age and background, the pair is a fascinating match, challenging each other with their high levels of virtuosity and playfulness to the great delight of the listener.

"Solo piano for me has always been a lonely pursuit," Corea says. "It only goes a certain way until I start missing the collaboration, because for me the joy of music is making music with others."[33]

LET'S TAKE A LISTEN TO "CRYSTAL SILENCE"

From *Crystal Silence* by Chick Corea and Gary Burton, ECM 1024 ST, 1973, recorded November 6, 1972, at Arne Bendiksen Studio, Oslo, Norway, with Chick Corea (piano), Gary Burton (vibraphone)

The first duet recording of Chick Corea and Gary Burton, *Crystal Silence*, released in 1973 on ECM Records became the soundtrack of an era and one of the first successful manifestations of an art form called chamber jazz.[34] The partnership came about as the two found themselves backstage together at the Munich Jazz Festival in 1972 with an enthusiastic audience that kept clapping for more music. They teamed up for an impromptu performance of Chick Corea's new composition "La Fiesta." Manfred Eicher, the owner of the German ECM label, was in the audience and realized the special connection of the two players. On his urging the two found themselves in the studio just a few months later. Manfred Eicher had reserved the Arne Bendiksen Studio in Oslo, Norway, for them for three days in order to provide ample time to rehearse and record.

They decided on a mix of originals and two compositions by frequent collaborators Steve Swallow and Mike Gibbs. In order to capture the spirit of the moment, the engineers turn on the recorders and the two master musicians seem to be reading each other's minds as they transform the raw song material into beautiful and melodic arrangements in mostly first takes. Only a short time into the session, Chick Corea suggests his ballad "Crystal Silence." A few months earlier, his group Return to Forever had recorded the song for their self-titled ECM debut. "Crystal Silence" features a beautiful melody framed with mostly A minor–based harmonies in a loose AABA format. Corea starts with little flourishes on the piano lining out the A minor tonality, and the beauty of the Norwegian landscape seems to move through his fingers as the time floats in and out and after a few bars he pauses on a beautiful B-flat major chord arpeggio. Burton immediately reacts to the cue and enters with the descending melody line. The first two vibraphone notes seem tentative—was my duet partner actually ready for me to come in?—but a quick look asserts that all is good and Burton introduces the melody, letting the long notes ring and vibrate. The tempo is still rubato and Corea follows Burton's melody notes quickly with the matching harmonic changes and quick-fingered arpeggios. Corea takes the lead at the bridge section, still in rubato mode, and Burton takes back the last A-section accompanied by floating piano flourishes. Corea loosely embellishes the harmonic progression of the A-section while Burton listens intently to the melodic landscape that Corea is painting. Now already five minutes into the recording, Corea establishes an impromptu two-chord vamp and a medium swing tempo. Burton joins and continues to display his improvisatory color palette on the vibes while Corea builds up the tension with the rhythmic vamp until Burton clearly states the last measures of the A-section melody. Listening intently, Corea immediately follows to the bridge section and reverts back to the floating rubato tempo. One final presentation of the haunting melody on the vibraphone decorated by Corea's harmonic landscape brings the piece to a close. A few more chords and the final arpeggio—another first take, everyone is nodding their head with approval.

The title track, a nine-minute exploration of Corea's beautiful ballad, displays a level of coherence and beauty that only two master improvisers can achieve. Building tension and release in the shape of a good story makes time disappear. Initially, the ECM label intended this project as a small release for artistic purposes but it continues to be one of the highest-selling albums for the label—a testimonial of the timeless and universal appeal that these two master musicians were able to create in only three short hours in Oslo's Arne Bendiksen Studio.

7

ACOUSTIC VARIATIONS

At the end of the 1979 school year a seventeen-year-old trumpet virtuoso in New Orleans who had just been selected to attend the elite Berkshire Music Center at Tanglewood made a written vow in his high school yearbook to "personally crusade against the 'bull—' of commercial music."[1] His father, jazz pianist Ellis Marsalis, had instilled a strong work ethic and drive for excellence in him, and by the following year Wynton Marsalis spent his time studying at the Juilliard School during the day and performing with Art Blakey's Jazz Messengers at night. His dedication to acoustic jazz and his ability to excel in both jazz and classical music generated headlines. Dubbed as "neoclassicists," Wynton Marsalis and several of his contemporaries modeled their music, their album covers, and even their clothes after the classic acoustic jazz of the 1940s to '60s before Miles Davis's electric crossover recordings and subsequent fusion of jazz and rock styles. His self-titled 1982 debut recording on Columbia is often cited as the beginning of the "re-bop" renaissance.[2] A group of young players, often dubbed "The Young Lions," "Neo-Classicists," "Re-Boppers," or "Wyntonites," with powerful support from major record labels produced a number of recordings rooted in the style of classic acoustic jazz; examples are guitarist Mark Whitfield, trumpeters Roy Hargrove and Terrance Blanchard, and pianist Marcus Roberts.

A wave of repertory orchestras signifies the neoclassic movement. The Lincoln Center Jazz Orchestra with Wynton Marsalis at its helm was founded in 1987 with an initial focus on reviving and preserving classic jazz repertoire. Similar groups followed, such as the Smithsonian Jazz Masterworks Orchestra under the direction of Gunther Schuller and David Baker in 1991. In addition to historically accurate presentation, Marsalis also insisted on the same level of preparation and stage presence as classical music; after all he was equally successful in jazz and classical music during his early career with back-to-back Grammy Awards in both genres in 1983 and 1984. The result was a remarkable improvement of the conditions for jazz presentations, whether in concert halls, recording studios, or nightclubs.[3]

The transformation of jazz into concert music and a renewed focus on acoustic music is reflected in Chick Corea's work during the years 1981–1985. Early in 1981, he recorded one of his most enduring collections, *Three Quartets*,[4] featuring Michael Brecker (tenor sax), Eddie Gomez (bass), and Steve Gadd (drums). Gomez recalled the recording process in a 2012 interview: "'We went out to L.A. for three days, we'd look at the music, play it a little bit and then turn the tape on. It was sort of like going out on a mission, like a SWAT team,' he adds with a laugh, 'because it was fraught with the danger of playing this new music, which I think in a way was really cutting-edge.'"[5]

The music was composed as chamber music pieces with the classic string quartet in mind but transferred to the sound and improvisational approach of a jazz quartet. The result is one of Corea's most enduring masterpieces:

> You know, that project was kind of a very straight shot because that suite of music played by that group of musicians was a unity in my mind. I thought of Steve Gadd, Michael Brecker, Eddie Gomez, and myself playing; and I thought, "You know, I'm gonna write a piece for us that is like chamber music, like a string quartet." That's why I called it Three Quartets. The string quartet is one of the classic orchestrations of chamber music, such a beautiful orchestration. And the saxophone quartet is one of the classic orchestrations of jazz. So I thought of it more or less as a piece of music written for this chamber group: I kind of combined the classical chamber music with the jazz quartet individuals I had in mind and wrote the suite of music in about a week and a half. It came out very easily because I could envision how one piece would move to the next, how one would feature primarily one player, then it would come around like this. . . . It was like a mini-suite, featuring these soloists and orchestra. The

> actual recording session only took two or three days. We had to rehearse the music just a little bit—there was some complexity in the music—but the quality and capability of those musicians was so high that with just a little bit of contact with the written notes, once they understood the forms, it just really started to roll down. After a couple of takes of each piece, we had it.[6]

For the original LP release, "Quartet No. 1" and "Quartet No. 3" appeared on one LP side and "Quartet No. 2" on the other due to time constraints. "Quartet No. 2" features two parts—one dedicated to Duke Ellington with colorful harmonies and tributes to Ellington's beautiful melodic writing, one to John Coltrane and his modal explorations. The group burns with intensity and especially Michael Brecker's masterful lines make the listener sit up and take notice. On the 1991 rerelease of the recordings on Stretch Records, four additional tunes add an extra bonus: the Corea originals "Folk Song," "Hairy Canary," "Slippery When Wet," and a rendition of Charlie Parker's "Confirmation."[7] Most likely these tunes were captured initially as the band was jamming in the studio and even feature Corea on drums swinging away on "Confirmation." The Quartets group was also captured during Corea's three-week celebration of his sixtieth birthday at New York's Blue Note and "Quartet 2, Pt. 1" is featured on the CD/DVD release *Rendezvous in New York*.[8]

In his introduction to the Three Quartets band at the Blue Note celebrations, Corea mentioned: "All my life, one way or the other, I've been steeped in European Chamber Music, Classical Music and I love that culture and tradition. And in one way or another I'm trying to merge them, the beauties of Classical Music and Jazz." While the chamber music concept of the "Three Quartets" pushes the stylistic boundaries similar to the principles of third-stream composers such as Ran Blake, Corea attempted a more traditional merging of classical music with jazz sensibility with the *Lyric Suite for Sextet*. The suite was recorded in September 1982 and released on ECM Records in 1983 and features longtime duet partner Gary Burton on vibraphone and a traditional string quartet in a seven-part suite. Seemingly inspired by Bartok's cycle of string quartets, most of the parts are through composed with occasional improvisations by Burton and Corea in selected pieces. Hence spontaneous interaction is limited to the vibraphone and the piano, thus creating the format of a concerto with the string quartet taking on the role of the orchestra.

Earlier that year, precisely on April 7, 1982, drummer Lenny White walked to the front of the stage at the Wolf & Rissmiller's Country Club on Sherman Way in Los Angeles and announced: "I'd like to take this opportunity to introduce you to the world's greatest musicians. On the tenor saxophone Mr. Joseph Henderson, at the keyboard Armando Chick Corea, on the acoustic bass Stanley Corbin Clarke." And Chick Corea added: "I would like to thank the wonderful friend and musician who put this whole thing together, Lenny White."[9] Just four days earlier this same group with the addition of trumpeter Freddie Hubbard had brought the house down at the Circle Star Theater in San Carlos, California, during a concert that was released later under the title *Griffith Park—Collection 2*. As Corea mentioned in the announcement, the project was Lenny White's idea and put together initially to back up soul star Chaka Khan's first venture into jazz. The straight-ahead session with Khan was released under the title *Echoes of an Era*,[10] an unfortunate marketing strategy as the famous singer does an excellent job interpreting this set of jazz classics and her name could have helped sell much larger numbers. Her skillful interpretation of Thelonious Monk's "I Mean You" is especially remarkable and the 1982 release did receive a Grammy nomination. Corea supplied the arrangements, most notably the signature horn unison lines on Gershwin's "I Loves You Porgy."

Unfortunately, Chaka Khan's management did not open up her schedule to join the group for a series of tour opportunities. As a result the group performed without vocals and eventually invited Nancy Wilson for a series of concerts. One of the live concerts with her was recorded at the Country Club live to two tracks on the earlier mentioned April 7, 1982, under the title *Echoes of an Era 2*.[11] A fun side story about this live recording is that due to bad weather in New York the band's luggage got lost on the way and everyone had to perform in their travel clothes, which were in Chick Corea's case a striped T-shirt and jeans.[12]

The group sans vocals recorded another studio set on the request of Elektra executive Bruce Lundvall, later president of the legendary Blue Note record label. He realized the wealth of talent assembled and requested an instrumental set to be released the same year.[13] The group did not disappoint and blazed through a collection of originals by the band members reminiscent of the recordings produced by Al Lyons on Blue Note during the sixties. A cassette recording through a mixing board during the subsequent five-date California tour was magically resurrected and mastered for the double LP *The Griffith Park Collection 2: In Concert*. As the night progressed, the passion and pure enjoyment of interacting on this collection of bop tunes with a group of superb players reached goose-bump intensity. In particular, trumpeter Freddie Hubbard was known for setting the bar high. Reedist Bennie Maupin opened his eulogy to Hubbard in 2009 with the following statement: "Every musician knew that if you were going to play with Freddie Hubbard, you had to be ready to be humbled."[14] This specific group lived up to the task and arguably confirmed Lenny White's announcement quoted earlier for their final concert on April 7, 1982. None of them wanted to miss out on this rare opportunity to just play.

In addition to the Griffith Park Collections and the classical crossover project with Gary Burton on *Lyric Suite for Sextet*,[15] Corea's collaborations in 1982 included reuniting with bassist Miroslav Vitous and drummer Roy Haynes for *Trio Music*,[16] the flamenco-based recording *Touchstone*[17] featuring guitarists Paco de Lucia and Al Di Meola as well as old friends Stanley Clarke and Lenny White, a new partnership with flutist Steve Kujala on *Again and Again*,[18] and the duet encounter *The Meeting*[19] with classical pianist Friedrich Gulda.

Throughout this flurry of activity with a renewed focus on acoustic settings parallel to the early eighties traditionalist movement spearheaded by the Wyntonites evolved another trend. The repertoire of especially the *Echoes of an Era* collections as well as the trio outings is rooted in jazz standards and the Great American Songbook. When asked about it during an interview with Chris Collins, Corea explains: "Yeah, it slowly dawns on us in the jazz world that we actually have a repertoire, just like the classical musicians have. We have a really deep repertoire of music that can be reinterpreted and reinterpreted and reinterpreted. It's a heritage that we've got: it's a legacy and part of our culture. A lot of jazz musicians are composers and write new music, but we've got this historical track that's so beautiful that you want to reinvigorate it every now and again, you know? You gotta hear 'Lush Life' every now and again, a new rendition of 'Perdido' or whatever."[20]

Interestingly the reunion with Roy Haynes and Miroslav Vitous, his trio companions from the 1968 landmark recording *Now He Sings, Now He Sobs*, features initially a Grammy-nominated double LP set titled *Trio Music*[21] composed of a record of free improvisations and a record of Thelonious Monk tunes. Asked about his relationship to Monk's music, Corea explained that he had an interest in his compositions from the very beginning. In fact, he had spent two weeks at the Apollo Theater performing opposite Thelonious Monk's quartet in 1959 and made sure to see every set. He continued to study Monk's music in depth especially once he started playing with drummer Roy Haynes, who had performed extensively with Monk and loved to talk about him and his music.

"From every composer (Monk, like Mozart, or like Wayne, or like Scriabin), there's something. . . . In order for me to play that music the way I would like to, there's something of the composer that I want to keep putting into it. So when I play Monk's music, I try to make it sound a little bit like Monk."[22]

More eclectic offerings followed until 1986, diving deeper into the intersections between jazz and classical music. Among them were two Grammy-nominated collaborations with flutist Steve Kujala on the ECM label. After the duet release *Voyage*,[23] Kujala and Corea tackled an ambitious five-movement suite titled *Septet*[24] featuring French horn and string quartet. Another ECM release is *Trio Music, Live in Europe*[25] featuring the free interactions and Monk interpretations of the trio live with Vitous and Haynes. And of course, Chick Corea published and recorded his collection of twenty piano miniatures titled *Children's Songs*,[26] which he composed between 1971 and 1980. Several of them have also been recorded in duet and group settings on various recordings.

Most notable about these further explorations is Corea's quest to create a common space between jazz and classical music. While this quest is certainly inspired by an artistic vision of elevating jazz as an art form and exploring new avenues, Corea also admits that the relentless touring schedule that is needed in order to interact with audiences and promote his music is a difficult lifestyle. Daily routines as a classical composer would certainly look different and be much more stationary. In an interview for *JazzTimes*, he mentioned: "Oh, sometimes I think I would love nothing better than to live a second life as a chamber music composer and write for string quartets, for duets, trios, and string orchestras. I once had an idea to take all my favorite soloists and write a solo concerto for each of them—like a solo concerto for Jean-Luc Ponty, a bass concerto for Stanley Clarke. But doing projects that large would require a whole other life, one that's quite different from the one I have now."[27]

A wave of third-stream composers, a term coined by French hornist/composer Gunther Schuller during a 1957 lecture at Brandeis University, have attempted to bridge the gap between classical and jazz music. Nevertheless, the traditional performance practice and performance spaces keep the two genres apart, that is, classical music is usually performed in concert halls while jazz is featured in small clubs and restaurants. Corea shares his perspective in a 1981 interview as he contemplates expanding his acoustic and classical crossover collaborations. "I'm trying to break down the barriers, actually, between jazz music and classical music. There's such a rich tradition and a rich esthetic in both areas that I love to operate in. I see no barrier myself, but, in the world, it seems that the way business goes, there are two separate circles. There are certain places where classical musicians perform and play . . . and certain places jazz groups appear, and never the twain shall meet."[28]

He certainly bridged many gaps during just five years with a total of fifteen recordings, a Grammy Award and four nominations, winning Composer of the Year in 1985 by the Europe Jazz Forum Reader Poll while crisscrossing among continents with small and large ensembles with his relentless touring schedule. And as the Wyntonites reached the height of their conservative quest in 1986 with the founding of Jazz at Lincoln Center and a host of repertory orchestras, Corea turned toward a new passion—synthesizers and technology.

LET'S TAKE A LISTEN TO "QUARTET NO. 1"

From *Three Quartets* by Chick Corea, Warner BSK 3552, 1981 vinyl, remastered CD Release Stretch Records SCD-9002-2, 1992, recorded and mixed January and February 1981 by Bernie Kirsh at Mad Hatter Studios, Los Angeles, with Chick Corea (piano), Eddie Gomez (bass), Steve Gadd (drums), Michael Brecker (saxophone)

At a time when jazz seems to be in a popularity crisis and young musicians with Wynton Marsalis at the helm proclaim a return to the roots, the disco wave is riding high, and the world mourns the untimely death of John Lennon, Chick Corea invites three current jazz masters to join him in the studio for a brand-new project. He is very familiar with each of the musicians from previous recordings and tours but the combination is new. As drummer Steve Gadd, Puerto Rican bassist Eddie Gomez, and saxophonist Michael Brecker arrive, Corea shows them his new compositions to be recorded over the next three days. After the success of his fusion group Return to Forever and a decade of touring, Corea's career is well established and he has the freedom and resources to experiment with new directions. Classical music, especially the music by Bela Bartok and Ludwig van Beethoven, had been a strong influence on him for a while and his vision for the new compositions is to transfer the intimate setting of a classical string quartet to an acoustic jazz quartet.

The four compositions are titled "Quartet No. 1, 2, and 3" with "Quartet No. 2" divided into two segments, one dedicated to Duke Ellington and one to John Coltrane. Corea hands out the music and the group rehearses the complex parts. It doesn't take long until everyone understands the format and a natural flow seems to be established. Corea nods to his trusted producer and engineer Bernie Kirsh, a collaborator for more than a decade now, and the tape is rolling. Corea plays the opening chords of "Quartet No. 1," an ascending rhythmic sequence, in unison with the bass. After a short pedal ostinato, Michael Brecker joins on the repeat of the theme with the tenor saxophone. As the rhythm section settles into a funky groove, Brecker improvises fills around the ostinato rhythms. The interaction grows in intensity and soon there are growls of excitement from the saxophone as the group finds its common plane of interaction and pulses in unison. Relentless melodic lines and figures float over the thickening rhythmic texture created by Corea, Gomez, and Gadd. Finally the group returns to the written score with a repeat of the opening unison sequence leading into a more relaxed piano texture. Now the bass takes the melodic lead soon joined in unison by the piano.

Two final strokes on the cymbal signal the conclusion of the written melody and the beginning of Gomez's bass solo. Brecker set a high bar of intensity and virtuosity just seconds ago and Gomez is determined to make his musical contribution special. His bass sound is quite characteristic with a thick, quasi-electric sound that was also featured on recent Corea recordings *The Leprechaun*, *Friends*, and *The Mad Hatter*. Drummer Steve Gadd settles into a modern swing beat and Gomez reaches into the upper register of his bass with a singing, vibrato-rich melody. In contrast to the earlier solo over an ostinato groove, the format now is a swinging 16-bar chord sequence with a concluding 4-bar A-minor segment in triple meter. Despite the unconventional harmonies and meter changes, Gomez lets his bass soar across five repeats of the form with beautiful melodies reinforced with added vibrato at the end of phrases. The listener is hypnotized by the intensity and dazzling display of virtuosity on a difficult instrument. Gomez repeats three bluesy notes and signals the end of his solo.

Corea takes over with a piano solo on the same 20-bar chord sequence. The rhythm floats initially, but by the beginning of the third repeat Gadd and Gomez are laying down a strong swing beat and lock in with Corea who settles into a long eighth-note line. The 4-bar triple meter endings of each chorus interrupt the flow throughout the eight repeats of the form. and finally Corea winds down with arpeggiated flurries. Brecker joins on the written theme for the middle section played earlier by bass and piano only. And fanfare-like, Corea returns to the opening chord cascade—similar to a classical piece when the initial theme returns. The group unites for a final unison coda, and with relief they let the last note ring. This is going to be the final take of this complex piece of music!

The mutual respect and enjoyment of this group of outstanding musicians shines throughout the whole recording and makes it such a masterpiece. In fact, the group had so much fun in the studio that they kept recording impromptu pieces when the *Three Quartets* were completed ahead of schedule. The remastered compact disc version that was released ten years later on Corea's own Stretch Records included three additional Corea originals and a jam of Chick Corea on drums with Michael Brecker showcasing his solo mastery on the Charlie Parker classic "Confirmation."

8

BACK TO ELECTRIC

"Is it live or is it Synclavier?" became a common phrase in the eighties as musicians explored the possibilities of this extremely sophisticated synthesizer and even mimed an entire show preprogrammed on the Synclavier.[1] The primary developers behind this new technology were Dartmouth professor Jon Appleton and New England Digital Corporation founders Cameron Jones and Sydney Alonso. The Synclavier system featured sound synthesis, sampling capabilities, hard-disk recording, and computer-based sound editing on such an advanced level that some concert halls even banned its use from their stages out of fear of making musicians obsolete. In addition to musical explorations by experimental musicians such as Kraftwerk, Laurie Anderson, and Frank Zappa, the Synclavier was used for audio analysis by intelligence services, military, and NASA and is still a common tool for film, TV, and commercial sound production. In the early eighties, Chick Corea became the proud owner of a Synclavier and started creating sequences and experimenting with its sound capacities and further uses of the sophisticated computer unit. But it still was a very complex system and not compatible with other units for onstage use.

In January 1983, at the annual NAMM (National Association of Music Merchants) Convention, Sequential Circuits' Dave Smith and Roland's Jim Mothersbaugh successfully connected two digital synthesizers from different manufacturers with one keyboard controlling the other.[2] The new communication tool between electronic devices in form of a five-pin connector cable called MIDI (Music Instrument

Digital Interface) enabled the transfer of information including pitch, duration, enhancements, and performance details. Through connection chains of electronic devices via MIDI cable, one computer or instrument could now effectively control the note and sound choices of all other connected instruments. For keyboard players this opened up a whole new palette of sound combinations as well as liberated them from having to set up racks of keyboards onstage. The invention of MIDI enabled an avalanche of new developments in portable keyboards, sound production, and electronic devices throughout the eighties. Especially notable was the 1983 introduction of the highly successful Yamaha DX series of MIDI synthesizers employing a new system of frequency modulation. Musicians in many genres experimented with the new sounds and technologies; for example, the Synclavier is featured on Michael Jackson's 1982 album *Thriller*, and synth pop groups became popular, notably the Eurythmics, Depeche Mode, and A Flock of Seagulls.

After a five-year whirlwind of musical activity ranging from classical to contemporary chamber music and numerous musical collaborations, Chick Corea felt the need to renew the connection to his audience with his own group similar to his seventies unit Return to Forever. In addition, he was experimenting with his new Synclavier, a Yamaha DX1, and a new MIDI-equipped Fender Rhodes Mark 5 similar to his contemporaries Herbie Hancock, Stevie Wonder, and Sting, and his old boss Miles Davis. Improving on the Return to Forever concept, Corea imagined a unit where each group member was involved in the musical decision making. "I wanted to create a musical life where everyone could flower without feeling confined in a group," Corea said hours before a performance in Poughkeepsie, New York. "The group should be something that should help everyone grow and feel free."[3]

Over the course of a year, Corea started to scout for a drummer and a bassist to form the new band. He recalled the process of choosing Dave Weckl and John Patitucci based on recommendations:

> Around '82 or '83, I started to want to form another group that had an electric sound to it, so I could write music kind of in the direction of Return to Forever, but with a new set of musicians. We were living in L.A. at that time, and my wife Gayle and I would put on Valentine's parties. . . . Gayle loves hearts and valentines, and so we would host a Valentine's party in L.A., and invite musicians and

> friends, just to come over. Gayle would always promote jamming during the evening. At that time, I was looking for a bass player. Gayle helped me find John somehow. I think he was playing with Victor Feldman. . . . Anyway, I found him on a cassette tape, and I thought, wow, this guy is great. He was invited over to the house, the Valentine's party, and I heard him play. Then I thought, "All I need now is a drummer." I wanted to start with a rhythm section. That was always a successful action for me, is to start with a rhythm section, no matter what kind of a band I wanted to build. Then the other fortunate thing that happened is that when I was in New York right after that time, I asked Michael Brecker, "who's the best young drummer around?" and without a lag he said, "Dave Weckl." I'd never heard of Dave. So we saw that Dave was playing with Billy Connors' trio down on the East Side there, and I went and saw Weckl play. He blew me away. I hired him that night. I said, "Can you come out and do these gigs?" That's how the Elektric Band got started. But John came along and just covered the whole . . . He's one of the few bassists I can think of, including Christian, too, Christian McBride. . . . John can cover all the musical bases, like Stanley can. That's an unintentional band.[4]

At the age of forty-five, Corea had now become a mentor to musicians twenty years younger in age. Similar to his opportunities with Blue Mitchell, Mongo Santamaria, and Miles Davis early in his career, he helped these young players refine their musicality and eventually launch solo careers. Initially the group started as a trio with a series of concerts and a repertoire of Corea's sketches. Patitucci recalls even getting Miles Davis's approval for the adventures at a festival; Miles was impressed by the innovative trio with the large array of keyboards.[5] Quickly it became clear that the voice of a guitar would be the ideal complement, and he invited Scott Henderson to join the group. He had noticed the young guitarist on recent recording projects with Jean-Luc Ponty and Jeff Berlin as well as by listening to Henderson's debut release *Spears* (Passport Records).[6] Corea added guitar parts and finalized the music and with the support of a five-year and seven-album contract with GRP Records, the self-titled debut album *The Chick Corea Elektric Band* was released in 1986[7] with additional guitar parts also by Carlos Rios.

Larry Rosen and Dave Grusin, cofounders of GRP Records (Grusin Rosen Productions), were ecstatic when the album became one of the best-selling jazz records of 1986 and garnered a Grammy nomination, thus making the new label an immediate success. Bassist John Patitucci describes the process of putting the music together as a group and Corea's mentorship: "We hadn't done any collaboration, any writing yet at that point. But we did his music and it was incredible and he would just bring stuff in with Dave and I first and it was like a workshop. He wanted to see what would happen with this new band. So, he was very open. He was very encouraging. He helped . . . he was just a great mentor. He allowed us a lot of freedom. The music was challenging but he opened the door for us to sort of run through it and find ourselves in it."[8]

For the follow-up release *Light Years* in 1987,[9] Corea added saxophonist Eric Marienthal, and Australian guitar wiz Frank Gambale replaced Scott Henderson. Actually, Henderson left the group after only six months and studio guitarist Jamie Glaser toured with the Elektric Band before Frank Gambale joined up just in time to record the second album. Glaser remembers getting a call to join the group in the middle of a Japan tour, apparently due to personal issues between Corea and Henderson. Glaser learned the very difficult music over the course of a few days and a plane trip to Japan and joined the group for the remainder of the tour.[10] Corea together with his longtime manager Ron Moss had implemented very strict rules for the band members about drug and alcohol use and it seems that those might have been the cause for friction with Henderson. In a 1990 interview, Ron Moss pointed out: "It's a straight band. They're alcohol-free and drug-free. It's a sane environment, not a crazy one."[11]

Light Years received a Grammy Award for Best R&B Instrumental Performance at the 1988 Awards. The approach was more cohesive and each musician was able to display his unique musical personality. "I'm too jazz for rock and I'm too rock for jazz, so I'm in this netherworld," Frank Gambale mentioned in a *DownBeat* magazine interview. "It used to bother me a lot more when I was younger. Now I know what I'm doing is important."[12] Corea also tailored his compositional approach to this new unit and the demands of a more commercial group. "I personally found it difficult to try and make an intelligent piece of music that only lasts four minutes. It was a strain. It didn't come naturally to me. Occasionally I'd come up with a piece, and it would be too short. That was a discipline. I wanted to see if I could keep the integrity of my message and intent and yet put it in a form that would get broader ears, and have more people experience the music. I also decided, in *Light Years*, to try and write songs that would keep a single rhythm from beginning to end, which I know is another thing that gives predictability to a listener and tends to keep them in the groove and interested rather than changing tempos and varying things, as I'm known to do. So I disciplined myself as a composer, and I found it an interesting thing."[13]

For the third Elektric Band recording, *Eye of the Beholder*,[14] Corea brought the acoustic grand piano back in the overall sound. "Without the acoustic piano, I felt incomplete, since it's my basic instrument and the instrument I express myself best on. I didn't want to have the acoustic piano and not have the other instruments, so I decided to confront the technical and production problem of incorporating it into the electric sound."[15] After two recordings and three years of deep explorations into the capabilities of the Synclavier and the MIDI-empowered Rhodes connected to various synthesizers, Corea felt drawn into a more acoustic sound mix. Furthermore, the acoustic sound was a better match to the group's interactive jazz mentality live and at recording sessions, where they usually finalized tracks in one or two takes. This specific recording is a fine document of the musical depth that can be created by a group of musicians who work together over an extended period of time and with music written with an understanding of each individual voice for such a group. Duke Ellington's band and musical leadership was one of the great examples for the level of artistry and unity that can be achieved by a tightly connected group of musicians with music written to showcase each individual's strength. Corea realized the potential of this group and implemented Ellington's concept successfully: "My role model is Duke Ellington in this regard. Not only did he write for his musicians, but he had a philosophy of life that placed value on the camaraderie and trust and the wonderful things that you can build up in a relationship over a period of time—the richness that can come to a relationship over a period of time."[16]

Being virtuosos on their instruments and versatile in many genres, the rhythm section of Chick Corea, John Patitucci, and Dave Weckl often performed in the traditional jazz piano trio format on acoustic instruments. In fact, their 1989 self-titled release *Chick Corea Akoustic Band*[17] featured the trio with a repertoire of standards and Corea originals and received the Grammy Award for Best Instrumental Jazz Performance, Individual or Group. Corea explains: "The other nice thing about the Elektric Band that I really enjoyed was the fact that the rhythm section—John Patitucci and Dave Weckl—within the group formed a trio that could play acoustic-style jazz, if you want to call it that, in the older tradition that I loved. Because I would get invites to do that while I had the Elektric Band, and I didn't particularly want to go out and form another band. So we did an experiment one time. I said, 'Dave, can you play a small kit of drums?' He said, 'Yeah, I'll give it a go.' Then John took out his acoustic bass and the Akoustic Band was formed."[18]

Of course, critics were skeptical about the trio's ability to interpret traditional jazz repertoire equally as well as contemporary fusion originals. Daniel Gioffre, in a review for *AllMusic*, claims that the band sounds "out of place" on the standards.[19] Corea explains: "The trio's first approach was not to think too much about repertoire. The initial idea was to play music spontaneously. I'd pick or write tunes that we'd rehearse, but they were sketchy, not highly arranged. The idea was to blow."[20] A second album by the Akoustic Band recorded live and aptly titled *Alive*[21] followed in 1991 and featured an array of repertoire by Duke Ellington, Billy Strayhorn, and Thelonious Monk, as well as some Great American Songbook selections and Corea originals. In a 1991 *DownBeat* article, Corea pointed out that instruments are tools for expression, communicating with the audience, and making music no matter if acoustic or electric.[22] "My goal is to send an audience home with some new ideas. And if they're the right ideas, if they're provocative enough, if they communicate effectively, they will hopefully trigger something that will encourage people to better experience their own creative lives. And I think that's something that's pretty worthwhile."[23]

These acoustic outings fueled the concept and repertoire of the Elektric Band. The mix of acoustic and electronic instruments already documented in *Eye of the Beholder* became a permanent feature of the last two albums of this group: *Inside Out*[24] and *Beneath the Mask*.[25] In fact, Corea's stage setup included an acoustic grand piano equipped with MIDI that triggered various synthesizers. Furthermore, the musicians were intimately in tune with each other after five years of constant touring and recording and easily switched between jazz-inspired swinging improvisatory segments and tight rock arrangements with complex unison lines. The rhythmically challenging selection "Kicker" on *Inside*

Out especially showcases the capacities and versatility of a group at its peak performance. Their artistry was awarded with two Grammy nominations in 1990: Best Fusion Performance and Best Instrumental Arrangement for the "Tale of Daring, Chapters 1–4."

The compositional process had evolved significantly by the final 1991 Elektric Band recording *Beneath the Mask*, or rather the final recording until the group reunited twelve years later on *To The Stars*[26] and then for a recent reunion tour. Various bass lines, melodies, and drum patterns are credited to John Patitucci and Dave Weckl on *Beneath the Mask*, indicating a more collaborative process. John Patitucci clarified in a personal interview: "And, then later on we did more writing too like on *Beneath the Mask* there's a few things that we wrote together. I think 'The Little Things That Count,' I actually wrote quite a bit of that. And there's other things too I can't remember. For 'Sidewalk,' I wrote the bass line."[27]

Throughout their decade of extensive touring and recording, Corea had also encouraged his band members to launch their own careers. In fact, he started his own record label, Stretch Records, under the GRP umbrella in 1992. From the early days of jazz, mentorship had always been a crucial element in learning and shaping careers. Beyond facilitating the musical development of his young colleagues through recording and touring with him, Corea hoped to provide the record label as a platform for their career development.

> Well, I had the model of Larry Rosen and Dave Grusin at GRP. They were two musicians who got together and made a record company. I thought, "You know, musicians should make record companies, because we're musicians. . . ." I've always enjoyed having the musicians, especially younger than me, who work with me . . . help them get their careers going. It's natural. That's how I would want to be treated when I was in a band. There's so much talent around. "Gee, let's do this." So there was funding available to do that. When I made my association with Glen Barros and John at Concord Records, that idea was right there. So we gave it a try.[28]

The philosophy of Stretch Records was to facilitate the artistic vision of the artist without commercial compromises, stretching musical boundaries. One of the first releases was John Patitucci's *Heart of the Bass*,[29] fulfilling his dream of making an orchestral record. Beyond providing the label support, Corea assisted also as a producer and arranger for Patitucci's solo outing. Stretch Records became the launching platform for a host of Corea's fellow musicians such as John Patitucci, Bob Berg, Eddie Gomez, Robben Ford, Avishai Cohen, and Eric Marienthal. In 1996, label consolidations marked the dawn of the digital age in the music industry. GRP Records became part of MCA Records and subsequently a subsidiary of Universal Music Group after the sale of Polygram. Corea decided to end his ten-year relationship with GRP and focus on his own Stretch label, now under the Concord Music Group umbrella.

Being a mentor to his younger band members also meant letting them move on as they were establishing their own careers as leaders. With the success of his Stretch Records release, John Patitucci decided to pursue new directions, and Jimmy Earl joined on bass for the last Elektric Band world tour in 1992 while Patitucci remained for a few Akoustic Band dates. Earl, a veteran of the Los Angeles studio scene, brought a new experimental spirit to the group, and with the other band members also ready to move on, Corea decided to scout for new band members. Recently a recording featuring guitarist Mike Miller had gotten Corea's attention, and a young drummer from Chicago, Gary Novak, impressed during a LA club performance. Corea invited Gary Novak and Jimmy Earl to jam at a local rehearsal hall and was impressed by the rhythmic chemistry. In fact, he adopted their spontaneity and openness as the guiding concept for the Chick Corea Elektric Band II.

The only remaining band member from the initial Elektric Band was saxophonist Eric Marienthal. *Paint the World* was recorded with first takes only after a few days of rehearsals and with minimal use of keyboards compared to the previous arsenal. Corea explained the concept of the new group in a 1993 interview with Zan Stewart: "If you don't know the music and you're using a second take to learn it, then you shouldn't be in the recording studio, you should be at a rehearsal hall. If you know the music and you're using the second take to do something better, you're invalidating yourself. If you continue that concept, then you might as well keep doing it for 14 years, and then you really get good and then you record *that*."[30]

With a meager 2.5-star review in *DownBeat* magazine,[31] the group was off to a slow start. Weckl's and Patitucci's virtuoso flights and the unique chemistry of the original Elektric Band set a high bar and could not be easily duplicated, although *Paint the World* received Grammy nominations for Best Contemporary Jazz Performance and Best Instrumental Composition. The Elektric Band II disbanded after their world tour and the original Elektric Band reunited for one more recording project based on the L. Ron Hubbard novel *To The Stars* in 2004.[32] The reunion project evolved naturally after the original Elektric Band performed a concert at the Hollywood Bowl and the deep chemistry reignited. Corea recalls the event: "'We toured and recorded a lot of albums. So when I got everybody together for the Bowl, it was like a bunch of old friends getting together. The repertoire came alive like that,' snapping his fingers for emphasis, 'so we started putting tours together. We did a couple of tours before I wrote new music for the band. But the band put itself back together.'"[33]

The new music became an homage to Hubbard's science fiction novel *To The Stars*, a book that Corea claims to have read at least ten times. While the music was inspired by the story, it's not supposed to be a soundtrack to the book but its own piece of art. Nonetheless, each composition is linked to specific quotes in the album cover. For example, there is the album opener "Check Blast" with references to pages 73–74:

> And then the light beam which shined in the distant nose of the Hound began to catch too many of its own particles back in its face too fast and the speed dial crept up to one hundred and eighty-four thousand five hundred. Alan spoke sharply to the communicator man: "Check blast five hundred." "Check blast five hundred, sir." And then, "Drives receipt check blast five hundred, sir."[34]

As the Elektric Band chapter came to a close, new acoustic ventures filled the last years of the twentieth century. Together with saxophonist Bob Berg and Elektric Band alumni John Patitucci and Gary Novak, Corea produced his last recording for GRP Records in 1995. Accompanied by an original short story in the CD booklet, *Time Warp*'s[35] selection "New Life" garnered a Grammy nomination for Best Instrumental Composition. As Corea was scouting for artists to join his Stretch label, he came across a cassette tape by Israeli bassist Avishai Cohen. He was intrigued by the creative approach and initiated a recording project for Stretch. While producing Cohen's recording, Corea was inspired by the artistry of Cohen's band members and invited them to form a new acoustic group called Origin. In a straight-ahead format with a three-horn front line, Origin released live sets from a weeklong residency at New York's famed Blue Note club in 1998 followed by the studio recording *Change* in 1999. What was initially planned as a demo recording effort with fellow band members Avishai Cohen (bass), Adam Cruz (drums), Steve Davis (trombone), Bob Sheppard (saxophones), and Steve Wilson (saxophones) became a box set release capturing three nights of creative excursions on six discs. In the 1999 *DownBeat* Critics Poll, the collection received the Jazz Album of the Year award as well as Jazz Acoustic Group of the Year award and Chick Corea was voted Jazz Artist of the Year.

Of course, reunions with duet partners Bobby McFerrin[36] and Gary Burton[37] as well as a tribute album to Bud Powell[38] also need to be included in the acoustic ventures between 1996 and 1999. But the final highlight before the turn of the century was the Grammy-winning live performance of Corea's first original symphonic work featuring Origin with the London Philharmonic Orchestra. *Corea.concerto*[39] includes his piano concerto composed in 1981 with Corea himself on piano and leading the orchestra as well as his arrangement of "Spain" *for Sextet (Origin) & Orchestra*. In a review for *AllMusic*, Judith Schlesinger writes: "This is the kind of intricate, multi-layered CD that sparkles brighter with each hearing; the 'Spain' arrangement alone is worth the price of admission. All told, it's more evidence of Corea's restless and brilliant talent; fans who've followed his winding artistic path for decades may well see this CD as a clear monument, if not a peak."[40] The effort was rewarded with a Grammy for Best Instrumental Arrangement—what a glorious start of the twenty-first century and with a year short of his sixtieth birthday the world seemed to be at Corea's fingertips.

LET'S TAKE A LISTEN TO "GOT A MATCH?"

From *The Chick Corea Elektric Band* by Chick Corea, GRP Records GRD-A-1026. LP 1986, recorded at Mad Hatter Studios, Los Angeles, with Chick Corea (piano), John Patitucci (bass), Dave Weckl (drums)

During a plane ride from Los Angeles to San Francisco, bassist John Patitucci watched Chick Corea scribble long strings of musical notes on a piece of paper. "What is this?" he asked. "Oh, you'll see later," Corea responded. The brand-new group with Dave Weckl on drums was preparing for their first recording at Corea's Mad Hatter Studios in Los Angeles. The trio had played several shows developing Corea's compositional sketches, and the new electronic setup centered around the versatile Synclavier and Yamaha's sensational DX keyboard series. The new programming techniques and MIDI (Musical Instrument Digital Interface) communication standard were still brand-new developments and had opened up a world of unique sound and performance options. One of the new tunes particularly suited for playing unison lines on the synthesizer is called "Got a Match." It has the harmonic framework of a minor blues extended to a 16-bar format. The melody begins with a D minor arpeggio sequenced over the first four bars followed by a similar motive over the G minor chord and then extends into a dazzling string of eighth notes. During the performances, Corea often uses the Yamaha KX5 keytar synthesizer controller and moves around onstage. Patitucci jokingly mentioned that he got himself in trouble by offering to play the melody along in unison on the bass.[41] Usually the group performs it at a speed of at least 240 beats per minute—a challenge for even a virtuoso like Patitucci.

As the trio sets up to record this particular song, Corea pulls out the music paper with the melody lines whose composition Patitucci had observed during the recent plane ride. It turns out that Corea envisioned additional extended unison lines to be performed by keys and bass during the drum solo. As Patitucci starts practicing the lines he realizes that they are even more complex than the original melody—and Corea had written all these lines on the plane off the top of his head![42] Now the challenge is to learn the difficult lines on the bass and in addition sync them up perfectly to the keyboard articulation as well as the improvised drum solo.

Engineer Bernie Kirsh gives the thumbs-up; the tape is rolling. Dave Weckl counts off and Corea improvises a melody line for one chorus lining out the song's harmonies. Here comes the theme—Patitucci takes a deep breath and joins Corea on the first D minor arpeggio in unison for the 16-bar head. Corea repeats the melody for a second time and Patitucci switches to a syncopated repetition of the chord's root notes for the first eight bars, then continues with a walking bass line. Everything is off to a good start and Corea continues with the keyboard solo. He is triggering a brassy synthesizer sound on the TX 816 module with the keytar that emulates the sound and phrasing of a horn solo. Of course, wind instruments only play one note at a time and have the ability to bend notes and change timbres with their embouchures. Similarly Corea performs the solo with one hand creating long single-note melody lines and uses the pitch bend controller with his left hand to bend notes and add vibrato to the sound. These types of techniques are not possible on an acoustic piano keyboard, and with practice time and experimentation onstage he has worked out a unique repertoire of pitch manipulations that facilitate the organic single-note melodies soaring in guitar-like fashion over the tight swinging groove of the rhythm section. Some of these techniques include creating grace notes by moving the pitch wheel up and back down, sliding up several pitches, ending phrases with an up or down bend, adding vibrato through pitch modulation, or purely rhythmic effects through stopped or bent notes with indefinite pitch.

For the first chorus at 0:42, Corea starts with a four-note motif and develops the idea into a closing 5-bar string of eighth notes. He takes a breath and then digs in deeper—the phrases are getting longer and more elaborate. At the beginning of the third chorus at 1:08, he pauses for three bars to collect his thoughts and positions his left hand on the slider to add some pitch bending effects toward the end of the chorus. Now he's on a roll and soars through a long bebop-type line followed by his characteristic rhythmic development of chromatically displaced two-note segments. The energy is high as he enters the final and fifth chorus with a phrase on the top end of the keytar keyboard at 1:33. He plays with the blues scale for three bars then continues the phrase downward for two octaves. One final rhythmic displacement game before pitch bending toward the final D. Quickly Patitucci joins to repeat the main melody at 1:45 in unison together with a slightly altered ending.

At exactly two minutes into the recording it's time for the bass solo. Patitucci moves into the upper registers of his six-string bass and Corea joins with melodic accents on the keytar for a dialogue into the second chorus. Over four more choruses Patitucci develops his virtuosic lines with Corea and Weckl accenting the harmonic outlines and chorus repetitions. Finally he plunges into a repeating three-note figure; Corea finds a sixteenth-note counter rhythm and moves it up chromatically on the keyboard, and Weckl joins the keyboard accents. At nearly three minutes into the recording, time seems to be suspended for eight bars with the band pulsing together in a parallel universe. The listener experiences the bass sound passing by with a Doppler effect before Corea takes charge and announces the end of the solo with the final two bars of the theme. He adds an improvised keyboard solo and turns it over to Weckl.

At 3:28, Weckl keeps the frantic eighth-note energy throughout his chorus with sparse cymbal accents, and Corea nods at Patitucci as they tackle one of the lines composed on the airplane ride. All three join together for a perfect rendition followed by one more drum solo chorus. The next line is designed as a dialogue, leaving space between the phrases for the drums to react to the rhythms. Weckl adds another solo chorus and, running out of written lines, Corea joins with two more improvised choruses before they all come together for the final rendition of the theme at 4:56 similar to the beginning arrangement. A final coda chorus culminates in a D minor keyboard cadenza and a held D minor chord bent up and back down. The intense focus and tension releases, and the group looks up with relief and nods at each other. They did it—they conquered another seemingly superhuman challenge with concentration and virtuosity!

9

SO MANY THINGS TO DO

On April 12, 2000, Metallica filed a lawsuit against the file-sharing service Napster. Two college students had unleashed a disruptive technology that caused panic across all sectors of the music industry. Just a month after boy group NSYNC broke their own first-week sales record with 2.4 million copies sold during the week of March 27, the recorded music industry descended into a downward spiral that is ongoing. The initial idea of the two young developers of Napster, Shawn Fanning and Sean Parker, was to create an online platform for their peers to swap music. In just a few months, the service had sixty million users and the two college students had managed to upend the traditional model of the recorded music industry, supplying income streams from recorded music to artists and their teams.[1] Napster was found guilty of copyright infringement but the cat was out of the bag, and similar file-sharing services followed. A new generation of consumers grew up with the expectation that recorded music is free and readily available anywhere and anytime. As a result artists had to focus on live performances and new patronage systems such as crowdfunding, subscriptions, and similar fan support models. Even a well-established artist such as Chick Corea found himself adapting to the digital age by broadening the range of activities and interaction with fans. This chapter traces Corea's projects and new approaches to touring and communication with audiences in the twenty-first century.

Most notable is the extraordinary amount of twenty-three releases over fifteen years winning thirteen Grammy Awards. Furthermore, each of these releases features a different project and different combination of personnel ranging from solo piano to various duets and trios, various incarnations of the Elektric Band and Return to Forever, new bands, to classical orchestras. When others are starting to think about retirement, at age sixty Corea's creativity and prolific output only seemed to increase. As noted earlier, this prolific output of releases came at a time when record sales dwindled and rarely offset the investment. In fact, Corea disbanded his own Stretch label, which became part of the Concord Music Group as it lost economic viability. In just a few years, the music industry model flipped 180 degrees with recording projects now serving as an incentive to secure a profitable touring career offset by merchandise sales. This last chapter presents a chronological overview of Corea's numerous projects for a final documentation of the breadth of his current career and the legacy of this living jazz legend whose creativity and artistry seems to have no boundaries.

1. THE CHICK COREA NEW TRIO: *PAST, PRESENT & FUTURES*[2]

The trio partners Avishai Cohen (bass) and Jeff Ballard (drums) were the heartbeat of the Origin band, and in the tradition of forming acoustic trios from group projects, Corea showcased these young players with a set of music specifically written for this rhythm section. Paula Edelstein describes the originals as "some of the freshest and finest compositions in Corea's career" in her review of the album for *AllMusic*.[3]

2. CHICK COREA: *RENDEZVOUS IN NEW YORK*[4]

These live recordings document Corea's extended sixtieth birthday celebrations at New York's Blue Note jazz club showcasing various ensembles and duo partners. Chick Corea turned sixty in 2001 and on the suggestion of Blue Note's manager Sal Haries, he invited many of his previous and current musical partners for a three-week celebration. Almost sixty hours of recordings with nine different lineups ranging from duos to small ensembles and from free jazz improvisations to a classical string quartet provided plenty of selections for a double CD release accompanied with extensive liner notes on the various ensembles and musicians. The nine ensembles are the Chick Corea and Bobby McFerrin Duo; the Now He Sings, Now He Sobs Trio with Roy Haynes (drums) and Miroslav Vitous (bass); the Remembering Bud Powell Band with Roy Haynes (drums), Joshua Redman (saxophone), Terence Blanchard (trumpet), and Christian McBride (bass); the Chick Corea and Gary Burton Duo; the Chick Corea Akoustic Band with Dave Weckl (drums) and John Patitucci (bass); Origin with Avishai Cohen (bass), Jeff Ballard (drums), Steve Wilson (saxophone), Steve Davis (trombone), and Tim Garland (bass clarinet); the Chick Corea and Gonzalo Rubalcaba Duo; the Chick Corea New Trio with Avishai Cohen (bass) and Jeff Ballard (drums); and finally the Three Quartets Band with Michael Brecker (saxophone), Eddie Gomez (bass), and Steve Gadd (drums). The album won a Grammy for Best Instrumental Solo in 2003 and was nominated for Best Instrumental Album and Best Instrumental Arrangement Accompanying Vocalists. The celebration concept was such a success that Corea's extended birthday residencies are now a Blue Note tradition.

Corea fondly remembers: "It came together in grand style with many of my good friends and treasured musical partners—all of whom I had the incomparable joy of making this music with over 3 weeks of the most incredible and joyous birthday party I ever had. The main joy though, was the joy of friendship in music. I began to reflect and measure the richness of my life in terms of the high value of the musical friendships I had after considering that, I realized that I was without doubt, the richest person in the universe."[5]

3. CHICK COREA ELEKTRIC BAND: *TO THE STARS*[6]

As discussed in chapter 8, this recording brought the group back together after ten years and is inspired by L. Ron Hubbard's science fiction novel of the same name. In addition to the core members Dave Weckl, John Patitucci, Eric Marienthal, and Frank Gambale it features guests Steve Wilson (sax), Pernell Saturnino (percussion), and vocalist Gayle Moran Corea.

4. CHICK COREA AND THE TRONDHEIM JAZZ ORCHESTRA: *LIVE IN MOLDE*[7]

Composer/arranger Erlend Skomsvoll led the Trondheim Jazz Orchestra with guest Corea through a set of reimagined and creative arrangements of Corea's music at the Molde International Jazz Festival in Norway in 2004. The project was made possible through funding by the Norwegian Arts Council as part of their "scheme for aspiring young people on the point of becoming professional artists" and is a wonderful example of cultural capital made possible through government arts funding.

5. CHICK COREA AND TOUCHSTONE: *RHUMBA FLAMENCO*[8]

This is a self-released live compilation of a tour with flamenco musicians Paco DeLucia, Carles Benavent, Jorge Pardo, and Rubem Dantas as well as drummer Tommy Brechtlein and special guest Gayle Moran Corea. Corea's deep love for Spanish music, reminiscent of earlier releases such as *My Spanish Heart*, shines throughout the compositions and performances. The album is only available through Chick Corea's website.

6. CHICK COREA: *THE ULTIMATE ADVENTURE*[9]

Similar to *To the Stars*, this recording is a tone poem based on the L. Ron Hubbard novel *The Ultimate Adventure*. Characters in the book serve as the inspiration for the various compositions, and the featured musicians are a mix of the Touchstone group and reunion with friends. The Spanish flavor is evident again with three percussionists, a combination of acoustic piano and Fender Rhodes, and some rare overdubbing where Corea duets with himself on both of those instruments. John Kelman describes the music in his review for AllAboutJazz.com as "challenging yet accessible, a perfect combination of head and heart."[10] The album earned Corea two Grammy Awards in 2006 for Best Instrumental Arrangement and Best Jazz Instrumental Album.

7. SUPER TRIO—LIVE AT THE ONE WORLD THEATER APRIL 3, 2005, FEATURING CHRISTIAN MCBRIDE AND STEVE GADD[11]

Corea refines the art of the trio throughout this post-2000 period by exploring various combinations of veteran and young players and creating opportunities to reunite with friends. On this particular recording he picks young bass sensation Christian McBride and one of his long-time partners, drummer Steve Gadd, for reinterpretations of his originals from the first fifteen years of his recording career. The group is in a playful mood and finely attuned to each other, and the energy of the live performance translates to a willingness to take risks and approach Corea's compositions with a fresh and adventurous perspective.

8. CHICK COREA AND BELA FLECK: *THE ENCHANTMENT*[12]

As discussed in an earlier chapter, this was a unique duo collaboration, crossing genres and musical approaches between the two musicians. The music was recorded in advance of extended touring and aside from the standard "Brazil" is a combination of compositions by Corea and Fleck.

9. CHICK COREA: *FIVE TRIOS*[13]

This is a six-CD box set only available as a Japanese import featuring five different trios and a bonus disc with additional tracks from each trio. Four of the trios were recorded live; one is a studio recording tackling repertoire from jazz and Brazilian standards to Corea originals. Throughout this period, Corea took an intense interest in the intimate interaction of the traditional piano trio and documented the various results. Each trio disc is also available under its project name:

Dr. Joe: Chick Corea & John Patitucci & Antonio Sanchez
From Miles: Chick Corea & Eddie Gomez & Jack DeJohnette
Chillin' in Chelan: Chick Corea & Christian McBride & Jeff Ballard
The Boston Three Party: Chick Corea & Eddie Gomez & Airto Moreira

Brooklyn, Paris to Clearwater: Chick Corea & Hadrien Feraud & Richie Barshay

10. CHICK COREA AND GARY BURTON: *THE NEW CRYSTAL SILENCE*[14]

Celebrating thirty-five years of collaboration, Corea and Burton released a double CD set featuring the Sydney Symphony Orchestra on one disc and the duo live at the Molde Jazz Festival on the second disc. Reedist Tim Garland shows off his brilliant symphonic arranging skills with settings of five Corea tunes for Symphony Orchestra, and the empathy of Corea and Burton reaches unprecedented heights. The artistry was rewarded with three Grammy nominations and a win for Best Jazz Instrumental Album in 2008.

11. CHICK COREA AND HIROMI: *DUET*[15]

Recorded live at the same place where Corea initially invited a seventeen-year-old prodigy to join him onstage for a duet, this performance at Tokyo's Blue Note captures pure joy and piano virtuosity. They tackle one original by each and a mix of standards and Beatles songs on this three-disc set.

12. RETURN TO FOREVER: *RETURNS*[16]

This collection features the highlights from a highly anticipated reunion tour of the 1970s fusion supergroup, at least one of the incarnations, with more to come over the next few years. Al Di Meola, Stanley Clarke, and Lenny White joined Corea for an extensive tour throughout the summer of 2008 also documented on a live DVD at the Montreux Jazz Festival. The tour was highly anticipated by fans worldwide and also took them to each member's hometown including Boston, where Corea's hometown Chelsea now has a street named in his honor.

13. CHICK COREA AND JOHN MCLAUGHLIN: *FIVE PEACE BAND LIVE*[17]

The recording is the culmination of a series of twenty-two concerts throughout Europe during the fall of 2008. Guitarist John McLaughlin is a fellow alumnus of Miles Davis's *Bitches Brew* project and fusion pioneer with his Mahavishnu Orchestra. The two jazz giants finally made their dream come true of having a band together and playing each other's music. Fellow Miles Davis alum Kenny Garrett joined on saxophone, with rhythm section Christian McBride and Vinnie Colaiuta as well as special guest Herbie Hancock. "I'm the perennial student," Corea says. "One of my private perks of all the projects I do is work with musicians I can learn from and grow from, and this bunch of musicians turned that out for me in spades, starting with John who is such a magnificent composer and has areas of music that he's created that I am quite unfamiliar with—his odd time signatures and Indian play with rhythms is something I don't know a lot about and I knew we would do a little bit of that. Plus wanting to work with the other musicians, play with them and be around them has been the main joy of these tours for me, to be in such a group and hear such creativity flourish every night."[18] *Five Peace Band Live* was selected as Album of the Year by *DownBeat* magazine in 2010 in addition to honoring Chick Corea as Jazz Artist of the Year and Electric Keyboardist of the Year, with the ultimate honor of inducting him into the *DownBeat*'s Hall of Fame—a grand slam.

14. COREA, CLARKE, AND WHITE: *FOREVER*[19]

The acoustic trio version of Return to Forever finally gets the spotlight for a tour of more than fifty live concerts. Special guests Bill Connors, Chaka Khan, and Jean-Luc Ponty join for several studio tracks on the second CD in preparation for the kickoff concert at the Hollywood Bowl, while the first CD captures the trio live at various club dates. Chick Corea, Stanley Clarke, and Lenny White initially performed together at the Keystone Korner in San Francisco in preparation of the electric version of Return to Forever that would soon fill stadiums after the release of *Hymn of the Seventh Galaxy* in 1973. Nearly forty years of collaboration were rewarded with a three-Grammy sweep at the 2011 Awards for Best Latin Instrumental Album, Best Improvised Solo, and Best Jazz Instrumental Album.

15. CHICK COREA AND STEFANO BOLLANI: *ORVIETO*[20]

This recording captures an improvised piano duo performance during the Umbria Jazz Winter Festival in Orvieto; only the song selections were planned. Corea has a long tradition of piano duo collaborations, and the two virtuosos shine and complement each other throughout the evening. The recording was released on the ECM label, closing a historic circle for Corea.

16. CHICK COREA: *FURTHER EXPLORATIONS*[21]

Recorded live at the Blue Note in New York City, this tribute to pianist Bill Evans captures one of the last performances of Bill Evans's longtime drummer Paul Motian in a trio setting with fellow Evans alum Eddie Gomez. It's a deeply emotional interpretation of some of Bill Evans's tunes as well as originals dedicated to his memory. Corea remembers Motian as a "walking, living, breathing work of art himself." Gomez calls him "the navigator" and "guiding light" of those two weeks at the Blue Note: "What might have been very special and beautiful, Paul took it way beyond that, into almost unclassifiable places. He was the force that took us there."[22] The listening guide at the end of this chapter for "Peri's Scope" documents this deep and emotional tribute to Bill Evans as well as one of Paul Motian's last performances before he lost his battle to cancer.

17. CHICK COREA: *THE CONTINENTS*[23]

Another double CD set with bonus materials of solo improvisations and jazz quintet performances on the second disc and Corea's composition in the spirit of Mozart on the first one. The concerto for chamber orchestra and jazz quintet is a six-movement suite named after each continent. The group conducted by Steven Mercurio, who also conducted the London Symphony Orchestra for Corea's concerto recording in 2000, is composed from members of the Harlem Quartet and Imani Winds with the jazz quintet featuring saxophonist Tim Garland, trombonist Steve Davis, bassist Hans Glawischnig, and drummer Marcus Gilmore together with Corea.

18. RETURN TO FOREVER: *THE MOTHERSHIP RETURNS*[24]

The year 2012 was not only the year with the highest amount of releases to date but each one seemed to get more elaborate. *The Mothership Returns* not only includes two audio CDs with more than one hundred minutes selected from more than two hundred live performances but also a DVD with two hours of footage including full-length performances and a documentary. Beyond the core group of Corea, Stanley Clarke, and Lenny White, this incarnation features violinist Jean-Luc Ponty and guitarist Frank Gambale plus extended versions of Return to Forever classics and two new originals by Ponty and Clarke. This clever strategy for connecting to fans through valuable packaging and providing unique content is a stellar example for shaping twenty-first-century music careers.

19. CHICK COREA AND GARY BURTON: *HOT HOUSE*[25]

This double-Grammy-Award-winning release marks the fortieth anniversary of the duo's collaboration. In preparation for this recording they agreed on a selection of eight of their favorite composers from the 1940s to the 1960s, resulting in a mix of American songbook classics, jazz and Brazilian standards, and Lennon/McCartney's "Eleanor Rigby." An extra bonus is Corea's composition "Mozart Goes Dancing," which features the Harlem String Quartet.

20. CHICK COREA: *THE VIGIL*[26]

The *Vigil* sessions brings together a new ensemble with completely new repertoire, and the cover features warrior Chick Corea in armor riding into the sunset on a unicorn. "Flood the market with music—refine the art of living—defy the existing norm—keep on creating: the mantra of the musician, the artist: Freedom of Expression."[27]

21. CHICK COREA: *SOLO PIANO—PORTRAITS*[28]

This double CD set combines solo versions of jazz standards, music by Scriabin and Bartok, and Chick Corea's *Children's Songs*, as well as a series of improvised portraits of audience members at various concerts. The portraits were released in conjunction with a whimsical limited collection of signed personal doodles titled *Creativity & Doodling*.

22. CHICK COREA: *TRILOGY*[29]

In the tradition of featuring a larger project's rhythm section in an acoustic setting, this release highlights the stellar rhythm section of the Five Peace Band with Christian McBride on bass and Brian Blade on drums. The repertoire is a mix of standards and Chick Corea classics. But most notable is the presentation in a three-disc format conceptualizing the title *Trilogy* from various angles. Furthermore, it won three major awards in 2015: a Grammy Award for Best Improvised Jazz Solo, a second Grammy Award for Best Instrumental Jazz Album, and the *DownBeat* magazine Award for Album of the Year—a true trilogy.

23. CHICK COREA AND BELA FLECK: *TWO*[30]

This 2015 double CD collection features selected concert segments of the duo with a combination of Corea and Fleck originals. Probably one of the highlights of the disc is their rendition of "Bugle Call Rag," successfully combining both of their virtuosity with the novelty of the banjo as a jazz instrument, thus combining a bit of the bluegrass roots into the improvisational explorations.

The year 2015 concluded with two more major awards. The Jazz Journalist Association named Corea Keyboard Player of the Year and *DownBeat* magazine honored him as Artist of the Year. Celebrating his seventy-fifth birthday in 2016, Corea hosted an unprecedented eighty-concert celebration at New York's Blue Note featuring all the facets of his career. The series included reunions of Return to Forever, the Elektric Band, Origin, and the Three Quartets Band, and, furthermore, concerts focusing on flamenco music, electronic experimentations, the music of Miles Davis, and various duets. The title of *Living Legend* is more than deserved at this point and we can all reap the benefits of an artist who seems to have unlimited energy and creativity to share with the world.

LET'S TAKE A LISTEN TO "PERI'S SCOPE"

From *Further Explorations* by Chick Corea, Eddie Gomez, Paul Motian, Concord Jazz, CJA-33364-02, 2-CD set, 2012, recorded at the Blue Note Jazz Club, New York, May 4–17, 2010, mixed at Mad Hatter Studios, mastered at Bernie Grundman Mastering, with Chick Corea (piano), Eddie Gomez (bass), Paul Motian (drums)

Pianist Bill Evans was known for his beautifully singing lines, impressionistic harmonies, and new inventive approaches to standards. He joined the Miles Davis Sextet in 1958 just in time to record *Kind of Blue* with the group, the best-selling album of all time. After he left the group, he led one of the most successful jazz piano trios with Scott LaFaro on bass and Paul Motian on drums, releasing four albums over just one year including the 1961 *Explorations*. Unfortunately, LaFaro was killed in a car accident shortly after the release at the age of twenty-five, a tragedy that deeply affected Evans, who struggled with depression and heroin addiction. Five years later Evans met a young Puerto Rican bassist, Eddie Gomez, which sparked new explorations and an eleven-year-long musical partnership. As a result of his ongoing struggles with addiction, Evans passed away at age fifty-one in 1980. The year 2010 marked several milestones—Evans's thirty years' passing and the approaching fifty-year anniversary of the release of *Explorations*.

Generations of pianists are deeply influenced by Evans's lyrical sense and beautiful sound on the piano, including Chick Corea. "Bill's harmonic sense and approach to the standards certainly made a big impression on me. I was more encouraged to produce a beautiful sound on the piano."[31]

In fact, Corea's friendship with bassist Eddie Gomez led him to brief meetings with Bill Evans in the late 1960s. When Evans's trio had a residency at the Top of the Gate club in New York, Corea would often come by and fill in during breaks or sit in at the end of the night. One evening Corea presented Evans with the lead sheet of a song that he dedicated to him titled "Bill Evans," which Evans politely accepted. Corea's intent with this tribute recording was the opportunity to play with Gomez and Motian, two exceptional trio partners, as well as honoring the musical legacy of Bill Evans.

In preparation of the series of concerts at the Blue Note, Corea had arranged some of Bill Evans's classics as well as added some of his own originals in the style or spirit of Bill Evans. Tonight, Evans's spirit seems especially present as the trio announces the next selection, Evans's original composition "Peri's Scope." Evans wrote the song for his black girlfriend Peri Cousins and initially introduced the song on the 1960 Riverside release *Portrait in Jazz*, just half a year after the release of Miles Davis's *Kind of Blue*—arguably the most influential album in jazz in part due to Evans's contributions. It's the first performance of this tune and Corea indicates to Motian to set it up on the drums with a swinging hi-hat beat—"You got it," he says with a laugh and Motian dives right in. After four bars of swinging he adds some accents on the tom—the audience has just started snapping along and laughs at the unexpected accents—there seems to be a bit of uncertainty on how long the intro was supposed to be, and after sixteen bars drums and bass join Corea on the melody of "Peri's Scope" accompanied by some cheers from the audience.

The most memorable feature of this Evans composition is a cross-rhythm figure in the melody during the ninth to twelfth measure, where the melody repeats a three-beat rhythmic figure five times for a polyrhythmic effect before settling back into the medium swing groove for the last eight bars. The tune also features a 24-bar through-composed melody, which is unusual compared to the traditional AABA song forms of the Great American Songbook. Corea's trio is well aware of the unconventional challenges, and as bar eight approaches at thirty-eight seconds into the song they easily slip into a three-beat groove, gracefully displacing the bar lines for four measures.

Corea takes the first solo while Gomez walks with a steady quarter-note feel and the whole audience seems to swing along. At the end of the first chorus Corea slightly alters the turnaround harmonies and at 1:20 switches into Corea mode with more percussive and precise rhythmic figures, the style he is known for. The three performers increase musical tensions with interactive figures and a deep swing that makes the whole room pulse in unison. Now in his third chorus at 1:46, Corea adds snippets from the original melody and a few figures reminiscent of pianist Thelonious Monk, thus paying tribute to the masters. At 1:55 Corea thickens the texture with triplet and sixteenth figures and Motian responds with offbeat accents just as they reach the cross-rhythm part of the chorus—again paying tribute to Evans by developing the original polyrhythmic figure. At 2:12 Corea moves into a fourth chorus supported by a press roll on the drums and finishes his solo accompanied by hollers and whoops of the audience. The trio trades four choruses of 8-bar units in various order and length of drum fills as the 24-bar form makes for uneven trading units. At 4:24 we hear the original melody one more time and with whistles and applause the audience acknowledges the improvisational capacities and the depth of the interpretation considering Gomez's and Motian's history with Evans as well as Corea's masterful leadership. It's not a perfect take—there are communication issues at the beginning as well as at the beginning of the bass solo and a raw and uneven drum sound—but the emotional quality takes precedence, capturing a deep-felt tribute to Bill Evans's music and mastery.

CODA

The Corea Legacy

In 2006, Corea received the highest honor for any jazz artist, the National Endowment of the Arts (NEA) Jazz Masters Award, a title bestowed yearly on a handful of legacy jazz artists, acknowledging outstanding musicianship and contributions to the art form. He now is one of our living legends due to his unparalleled level of creativity, prolific output, virtuosic mastery of the piano and numerous prestigious awards. His influence reaches far beyond jazz into all styles of music as a model for innovation, talent, and dedication. With 250-plus tour dates per year around the world ranging from solo piano to large fusion ensembles, he certainly doesn't have the time and need to teach private lessons and workshops. But the virtual world now provides opportunities to interface with fans and students all over the world and communicate instantly. Chick Corea's website is a model for twenty-first-century audience engagement and various options to connect beyond physical venues. Here are a few of the interactive features:

1. Fans can sign up on the mailing list and frequently receive private invitations to send in questions for upcoming online workshops and special package offers as well as tour announcements. Of course, frequent news is also shared through social networking sites, with close to five hundred thousand likes on Facebook alone.

2. The *Music Magic* podcasts include conversations of Corea with fellow musicians about their music and philosophies and just sharing memories. They provide glimpses into the tour bus, the airport, backstage, and the recording studio and bring the legends of jazz closer to their audiences.
3. For musicians, the online music workshops and master classes mostly presented live provide opportunities to send in questions and learn from the masters. Musicians can sign up for a fee and after the initial live broadcast the workshops are archived for later access. Participants register and tune in from all over the world and come together as a community.
4. The website, featuring a detailed discography, historical timeline, awards listings, picture galleries, and even transcripts from recent interviews provides a treasure trove of information for audiences and prospective collaborators. The various features bring together a community of fans and future audiences and keep them engaged through frequent additions of new content and bonus materials.

Very few jazz artists engage with their audiences on a similar level as Corea. Communication with the audience became a guiding principle for creating his group Return to Forever half a century earlier, and Corea has stayed true to his principles ever since. Drummer Brian Blade of the multi-Grammy-winning configuration Trilogy recently noted: "It's the heart of the man—the way he embraces people . . . and exhorts, encourages and inspires them, and those qualities come out in his playing. That beautiful 'crystal silence.' The clarity with which he executes lines and the way he presents and plays from his imagination. He's never resting on yesterday's decorations, he's always looking for another doorway."[1]

Beyond just communicating, Corea has very strong feelings about music education. He believes in guiding students toward finding their own voice and strength beyond gathering the needed tools and knowledge. In a 2014 *DownBeat* article he expresses his educational philosophy:

> Education in music is important but extremely misunderstood. You can't teach someone to know or appreciate something, or to know what they like, no matter how much data you give them. You could

> read every book in the library and still not know anything: that's what I think. [Musicians] know what they like. But you have to encourage them to have the strength of their own conviction, to live the truth of what they like and don't like.
>
> The word like may sound like a weak word, but that's how an artist makes a decision. How do you write a song or paint a painting? Well, you put something down that you "like," that you think works. No one can instruct you how to reach that decision. When you try, it invalidates their innate knowingness. So, "instruction" in music is very tricky. If it's done with an authoritarian stance—like, this is right and this is wrong—it could destroy a young artist. You can teach techniques though. Even that is tricky, because each artist has to find the technique that he needs to develop what's inside him. I'd like to help more artists and encourage more artistic creation. We need more musicians to lift our spirits around the world.[2]

The ultimate student himself, Corea continues his quest for creative expression, validated by the artists' ability to interact and communicate according to Corea's philosophy, thus dictating any technical needs. Other contemporary artists put very little emphasis on the interactive aspects with the audience and rather focus on their personal expressive needs. One prominent example is Keith Jarrett, who requests absolute silence from his listeners and has been known to stop performing in reaction to audience noises. Also, Glenn Gould eventually refrained from any public performances to attain the highest musical quality. Corea describes his process of continued self-improvement in a conversation with educator Chris Collins: "That's the only thing I ever try and change about myself: to improve my ability to interact and communicate. Based on that, I get ideas of how I want to do the mechanical part of it, how I want to write music, or whatever."[3]

Furthermore, Corea advocates the healing power of the arts by engaging in the artistic process. Becoming involved at any level provides a channel for expressing emotions and communicating beyond words. Quality and locality are not necessarily defining criteria for meaning. In fact, creating art is an essential aspect of living. "Where a musician goes—big city or small town—is secondary: the achievement of our artistic goals is a subjective and personal thing. Everyone will have a different mix in their lives as to how they use art. You could say there are a lot of 'non-professional' artists: mothers, businessmen, people in different walks of life who appreciate art, who love to create art in their lives by creating a beautiful home or having an artistic view of life. I mean you can live life as an art form. I think it's very confining to think of 'art' as a profession only: like being a trumpet player or piano player [is the only way to be an artist]—very, very limited view."[4]

Chick Corea is certainly an exceptional source of creativity, vision, talent, and seemingly endless energy as he continues to engage in the process of creating music and communicating with audiences on a personal and virtual level. His legacy beyond the extensive body of compositions, recordings, and lasting memories is the pure joy of engaging in the improvisational process in an interactive and meaningful way as a model for all our human interactions and realizing our dreams.

> The world is headed where we make it head. The future is in our minds. It's not in the physical universe. The future is what we intend, what we dream, and what we then resolve to do. The future is where our hopes are. The future is what we look forward to, to make happiness for ourselves. We have to be willing to invent something new in the future. You review the past and say. "That was great, but this wasn't so good, so now I'm gonna try it another way." Now you've pointed your face to the future.[5]

NOTES

INTRODUCTION

1. Ted Panken, Smithsonian Jazz Oral History Program NEA Jazz Masters interview with Armando Anthony "Chick" Corea, p. 4, November 5, 2012, Archives Center, National Music of American History, Washington, DC.

2. Stuart Isacoff, *A Natural History of the Piano* (New York: Knopf, 2011), 184.

3. James Lester, *Too Marvelous for Words: The Life and Genius of Art Tatum* (New York: Oxford University Press, 1995), 76.

4. David Meltzer, ed., *Writing Jazz* (San Francisco: Mercury House, 1999), 203.

5. Josef Woodard, "Chick Corea: The Next Chapter," *Jazz Times* 27, no. 2 (March 1997): 38.

1. *NOW HE SINGS, NOW HE SOBS*— WHAT WAS?

1. Ted Panken, Smithsonian Jazz Oral History Program NEA Jazz Masters interview with Armando Anthony "Chick" Corea, p. 1, November 5, 2012, Archives Center, National Music of American History, Washington, DC.

2. Ibid.

3. *The Thing to Do*, Blue Note BST 84178, Blue Mitchell (trumpet), Junior Cook (tenor saxophone), Chick Corea (piano), Gene Taylor (bass), Al Foster (drums). Van Gelder Studio, Englewood Cliffs, NJ, July 30, 1964.

4. Personal interview with Gene Perla, January 10, 2015.

5. Pete La Roca, *Turkish Women at the Bath*. Recorded in NYC, May 25, 1967. Originally issued on Douglas SD 782, featuring John Gilmore (tenor saxophone), Chick Corea (piano), Steve Swallow (bass), Pete La Roca (drums).

6. Panken, interview with Chick Corea, 9.

7. Chick Corea, *Tones for Joan's Bones*, recorded at Atlantic City Studios, NYC, November 30 / December 1, 1966, released on Atlantic/Vortex 1967.

8. Harvey Pekar, review of *Tones for Joan's Bones*, *DownBeat* 35, no. 25 (1968): 23.

9. Ornette Coleman's release *Free Jazz: A Collective Improvisation*, Atlantic SD 1364, 1961, features a double quartet and the first album-length free improvisation and was considered a milestone in free jazz explorations.

10. Interview with All About Jazz, August 2009.

11. A scale constructed exclusively of whole steps (a movement of two keys on the piano keyboard), which makes for a completely neutral tonality.

12. T. Rosenthal. (1998, 01). "Freedom and taste." *Piano & Keyboard*, 28–34.

2. *BITCHES BREW* AND *IN A SILENT WAY*

1. More details in Paul Tingen, *Miles Beyond: The Electric Explorations of Miles Davis, 1967–1991* (New York: Billboard Books, 2001), 50.

2. Originally released on LP 1970 Vanguard VSD 6558.

3. Originally released on LP 1968 Solid State SR 3157.

4. Originally released on two separate LPs, 1969, *Emergency! Vol. 1* (Polydor 24-4017) and *Emergency! Vol. 2* (Polydor 24-4018).

5. More info on the Grateful Dead in Bill Knight, "Grateful Dead (Music Group)," *Salem Press Encyclopedia* Research Starters, 2015, EBSCOhost, accessed May 26, 2015.

6. In Michael Veal, "Miles Davis's Unfinished Electric Revolution," *Raritan* 22, no. 1 (2002): 159. Art Source, EBSCOhost, accessed May 26, 2015.

7. Miles Davis, *In a Silent Way*, with Chick Corea, Herbie Hancock, John McLaughlin, Wayne Shorter, Dave Holland, Tony Williams, © 1969, 1969 by Columbia CS 9875, vinyl.

8. Tingen, *Miles Beyond*, 60. Tingen uses the expression "tone poem" and attributes Stanley Crouch with the term "droning wallpaper music."

9. According to the title of Dan Ouelette's detailed account, "*Bitches Brew*: The Making of the Most Revolutionary Jazz Album in History," *DownBeat* 66, no. 12 (1999): 32–34, 36–37.

10. Miles Davis, *Bitches Brew*, with Chick Corea, Harvey Brooks, Don Alias, Jack DeJohnette, Lenny White, Dave Holland, John McLaughlin, Bennie

Maupin, Joe Zawinul, Larry Young, Wayne Shorter, © 1970, 1970 by Columbia GP 26, 2 x vinyl.

11. Tingen, *Miles Beyond*, 57.
12. Ibid., 58.
13. "John McLaughlin," *Guitar Player* 26, no. 1 (January 1992): 79.
14. Ouellette, "*Bitches Brew*," 34.
15. Ibid., 36.
16. Ibid.

3. CIRCLE—AN AVANT-GARDE EXCURSION

1. Monika Herzig, *David Baker: A Legacy in Music* (Bloomington: Indiana University Press, 2011), 30.

2. Interview with bassist Larry Ridley by Monika Herzig, January 11, 2010, at his home.

3. Charlie Haden provides a detailed account of the making of free jazz in the chapter "Free Jazz Revisited" in Robert Walser, *Keeping Time: Readings in Jazz History* (New York: Oxford University Press, 2014), 320.

4. Released September 1961, *Free Jazz—A Collective Improvisation* by the Ornette Coleman Double Quartet, Atlantic SC 1364.

5. More on the impact of this group in Michael Veal, "Miles Davis's Unfinished Electric Revolution," *Raritan* 22, no. 1 (2002): 153–63.

6. Released July 17, 2001, *Live at the Fillmore East, March 7, 1970: It's about That Time*, Columbia/Legacy.

7. Thom Jurek, review of *The Complete "Is" Sessions*, AllMusic.com, n.d., http://www.allmusic.com/album/the-complete-is-sessions-mw0000226346.

8. See Chick Corea discography for more details: http://chickcorea.com/discography/.

9. Geoff Andrew, "Picturing New Sounds," *Aesthetica* no. 63 (2015): 134.

10. A detailed account of Manfred Eicher's work with ECM can be found in the forty-year celebration book by Steve Lake and Paul Griffiths, eds., *Horizons Touched: The Music of ECM* (London: Granta Books, 2007).

11. The recording was released under the title *A.R.C.* on ECM 1009 in 1971.

12. Vladimir Bogdanov, Chris Woodstra, and Stephen Thomas Erlewine, *All Music Guide: The Definitive Guide to Popular Music* (San Francisco: Backbeat Books/All Media Guide, 2001), 1198.

13. John Toner, "Chick Corea," *DownBeat* 41, no. 6 (1974): 15.

14. Philip Booth, "Sketching a Perfect Circle," *Jazziz* 15, no. 12 (December 1998): 47.

15. The case is documented in detail in Greg Taylor, "Scientology in the German Courts," *Journal of Law and Religion* 19, no. 1 (2003–2004): 153–98.

16. Foreword in Bill Dobbins, transcriber. *Chick Corea Piano Improvisations*. Rottenburg, Germany: Advance Music, 1990.

17. Chick Corea, "The Function of an Artist, Part 2," *DownBeat* 40, no. 9 (1973): 15.

18. The album reached No. 8 on the Billboard Top Jazz Albums charts in 1968. *Nefertiti* was reissued in 1998 by Columbia and Legacy Records (catalog number CK-65681).

4. RETURN TO FOREVER— THE ACOUSTIC YEARS

1. Lee Underwood, "Chick Corea: Soldering the Elements, Determining the Future," *DownBeat* 43, no. 17 (October 1976): 47.

2. As expressed in Michael Dwyer, "Chick Corea's '70s Jazz Group Return to Forever Is Back," *Sydney Morning Herald*, February 7, 2011.

3. Eric Nemeyer, "Chick Corea," *Jazz Inside* 3, no. 7 (February 2002): 14.

4. Andy Robson, "Blast from the Past," *Jazzwise*, no. 122 (August 2008): 26.

5. In-depth biographies for the musicians in the initial Return to Forever group can be found in the *Oxford Dictionary of Music Online*, http://www.oxfordmusiconline.com/public/book/omo_t237.

6. The story was reported in Stuart Nicholson, "To Infinity and Beyond," *Jazzwise*, no. 95 (March 2006): 36–39.

7. Thom Jurek, review of *Captain Marvel*, AllMusic.com, n.d., http://www.allmusic.com/album/captain-marvel-mw0000045641.

8. Chick Corea, *Return to Forever*, with Return to Forever, © 1972, 1972 by ECM Records 78118 21022 - 4, vinyl.

9. Chick Corea, *Light as a Feather*, with Return to Forever, © 1973, 1973 by Polydor 2310 247, vinyl.

10. Robson, "Blast from the Past," 26.

11. The album was released on Columbia Records in 1960 under the title of *Sketches of Spain*, produced by Teo Macero and Irving Townsend. The album opens with an extensive arrangement by Gil Evans of the adagio movement of the *Concierto de Aranjuez* by the contemporary Spanish composer Joaquin Rodrigo. The Davis recording includes very little improvisation and has often been criticized for including too few jazz elements.

12. Alex Hoyt,. "How Chick Corea Wrote 'Spain.'" *Atlantic*, November 25, 2011.

5. RETURN TO FOREVER—ELECTRIC

1. Chick Corea, *Hymn of the Seventh Galaxy*, with Return to Forever, © 1973, 1973 by Polydor PD 5536, vinyl.

2. Daniel Gioffre, review of *Hymn of the Seventh Galaxy*, AllMusic.com, n.d., http://www.allmusic.com/album/hymn-of-the-seventh-galaxy-mw0000263493.

3. Jurg Solothurnmann, "Chick Corea: Feel the Joy of Life," *Jazz Forum*, no. 34 (1975): 52.

4. Walter Kolosky, *Power, Passion and Beauty: The Story of the Legendary Mahavishnu Orchestra; The Greatest Band That Ever Was* (Cary, NC: Abstract Logix Books, 2006), 134.

5. Chick Corea, "Musicmagic," with Return to Forever. © 1977, 1977 by Columbia PC 34682, vinyl.

6. Jurg Solothurnmann, "Chick Corea: Feel the Joy of Life," *Jazz Forum*, no. 34 (1975): 51.

7. Chick Corea, *Light as a Feather*, with Return to Forever, © 1973, 1973 by Polydor 2310 247, compact disc.

8. Chick Corea, "Hymn of the Seventh Galaxy," with Return to Forever. © 1973, 1973 by Polydor PD 5536, vinyl.

9. Jurg Solothurnmann, "Chick Corea: Feel the Joy of Life," *Jazz Forum*, no. 34 (1975): 52.

10. Andy Robson, "Blast from the Past," *Jazzwise*, no. 122 (August 2008): 26.

11. John Runcie, "Chick Corea: Portrait of the Artist as Communicator," *Jazz Journal* 29, no. 8 (August 1976): 27.

12. Willard Jenkins, "Fusion Warriors," *DownBeat* 73, no. 5 (May 2006): 48.

13. Ibid.

14. Berthold Klostermann, "Chick Corea Forever," *Fono Forum*, July 2011, 53.

15. James Hale, "Bill Connors: New Identity," *DownBeat* 72, no. 4 (2005): 34.

16. Robson, "Blast from the Past," 27.

17. Ibid.

18. Anil Prasad, "Al Di Meola: Telling It Like It Is," Innerviews, 2003, retrieved February 19, 2016, http://www.innerviews.org/inner/dimeola.html.

19. Chick Corea, *Where Have I Known You Before*, with Return to Forever, © 1974, 1974 by Polydor PD 6509, compact disc.

20. Chick Corea, *No Mystery*, with Return to Forever, © 1975, 1975 by Polydor PD 6512, vinyl.

21. Chick Corea, *Romantic Warrior*, with Return to Forever, © 1976, 1976 by Columbia PC 34076, vinyl.

22. Hale, "Bill Connors," 35.

23. Jenkins, "Fusion Warriors," 48.

24. Personal interview by the author with Lenny White conducted September 12, 2016.

25. Chick Corea, *The Leprechaun*, with Joe Farrell, Anthony Jackson, Eddie Gomez, Steve Gadd, © 1976, 1976 by Polydor PD 6062, vinyl.

26. Chick Corea, *Musicmagic*, with Return to Forever, © 1977, 1977 by Columbia PC 34682, vinyl.

27. Chick Corea, *The Best of Return to Forever*, with Return to Forever, © 1980, 1980 by Columbia JC 36359, vinyl.

28. Corea, *The Leprechaun*.

29. Chick Corea, *My Spanish Heart*, with Stanley Clarke, Steve Gadd, Don Alias, © 1976, 1976 by Polydor PD-2-9003, vinyl.

30. Chick Corea, *The Mad Hatter*, with Herbie Hancock, Eddie Gomez, Steve Gadd, © 1978, 1978 by the Mad Hatter PD-1-6130, vinyl.

31. Chick Corea, *Friends*, with Joe Farrell, Eddie Gomez, Steve Gadd, © 1978, 1978 by Polydor PD-1-6160, vinyl.

32. Chick Corea, *Secret Agent*, with Joe Farrell, Bunny Brunel, Tom Brechtlein, © 1978, 1978 by Polydor PD-1-6176, vinyl.

33. Chick Corea, *Tap Step*, with Bunny Brunel, Joe Farrell, Tom Brechtlein, © 1980, 1980 by Warner Bros. Records BSK 3425, vinyl.

34. Thom Jurek, review of *My Spanish Heart*, AllMusic.com, n.d., http://www.allmusic.com/album/my-spanish-heart-mw0000016545

35. Juan Zagalaz, "The Jazz-Flamenco Connection: Chick Corea and Paco de Lucia between 1976 and 1982," *Journal of Jazz Studies* 8, no. 1 (Spring 2012): 44.

36. Lee Underwood, "Armando in Wonderland," *DownBeat*, March 1978, 14–15.

37. Ibid.

38. Ibid.

39. Chick Corea, *An Evening with Herbie Hancock & Chick Corea: In Concert*, with Herbie Hancock, © 1978, 1978 by Columbia PC2 35663, vinyl.

40. Chick Corea, *Return to Forever—Live*, with Return to Forever, © 1978, 1978 by Columbia, Columbia C4X 35350, 4 x vinyl.

41. John Kelman, review of *Secret Agent*, AllAboutJazz.com, June 26, 2006, http://www.allaboutjazz.com/secret-agent-chick-corea-universal-music-japan-review-by-john-kelman.php.

42. Ibid.

43. Chick Corea, *Tap Step*, with Bunny Brunel, Joe Farrell, Tom Brechtlein, © 1980, 1980 by Warner Bros. Records BSK 3425, vinyl.

44. Record reviews: *Tap Step*. (1980, September). *Downbeat*, 4746.

45. Chick Corea, *Return to Forever Returns*, with Return to Forever, © 2008, 2008 by Eagle Rock Entertainment ER 20149-2, compact disc.

46. Peter Watrous, "Thirty Years of Our Jazz Times: The 90s," *JazzTimes*, September 1, 2000, http://jazztimes.com/articles/20307-thirty-years-of-our-jazztimes-the-90s.

47. Lee Jeske, "Chick Corea," *DownBeat* 48, no. 6 (June 1981): 16–19.

48. Mike Haid, "A Conversation with Chick Corea," *Music Connection* 21, no. 10 (1997): 28–33.

49. Personal interview by the author with Lenny White conducted September 12, 2016.

50. Josef Woodard, "Kiss My Assets: Al Di Meola," *DownBeat* 59, no. 1 (January 1992): 23.

51. As published in Ernie Rideout, "Where Have We Heard Them Before? Chick Corea and Return to Forever Reunite to Remind Us of Some of the Greatest Fusion Ever," *Keyboard*, July 2008: 24ff. Biography in Context, accessed February 26, 2016.

6. PLAYING WITH FRIENDS

1. Gene Armstrong, "Decades as a Duo: Gary Burton and Chick Corea Bring 41 Years of Collaboration to the Fox," *Tucson Weekly*, January 17, 2013.

2. Ted Panken, Smithsonian Jazz Oral History Program NEA Jazz Masters Interview with Armando Anthony "Chick" Corea, p. 19, November 5, 2012, Archives Center, National Music of American History, Washington, DC.

3. Chick Corea, *Crystal Silence*, with Gary Burton, © 1973, 1973 by ECM Records ECM 1024 ST, vinyl.

4. Armstrong, "Decades as a Duo."

5. Armstrong, "Decades as a Duo."

6. Corea, *Crystal Silence.*

7. Chick Corea, *Duet*, with Gary Burton, © 1979, 1979 by ECM Records ECM M5E 1140, vinyl.

8. Chick Corea, *In Concert, Zürich, October 28, 1979*, with Gary Burton, © 1980, 1980 by ECM Records ECM-2-1182, 2 x vinyl.

9. Chick Corea, *Native Sense*, with Gary Burton, © 1997, 1997 by Stretch SCD-9014-2, compact disc.

10. Chick Corea, *Like Minds*, with Gary Burton, Roy Haynes, Dave Holland, Pat Metheny, © 1998, 1998 by Concord Records, Concord Jazz CCD-4803-2, compact disc.

11. Chick Corea, *The New Crystal Silence*, with Gary Burton, © 2008, 2008 by Concord Records CCD2-30630, compact disc.

12. Chick Corea, *Hot House*, with Gary Burton, Harlem String Quartet, © 2012, 2012 by Concord Records CIA-33363-02, compact disc.

13. Panken, interview with Chick Corea, 30.

14. In Eric Nemeyer, "Chick Corea," *Jazz Inside* 3, no. 7 (February 2002).

15. John Shand, "Chick Corea and Herbie Hancock Review: Extraordinarily Liquid Music That Will Live in the Memory," *Sydney Morning Herald*, June 2, 2015, http://www.smh.com.au/entertainment/music/chick-corea-and-herbie-hancock-review-extraordinarily-liquid-music-that-will-live-in-the-memory-20150602-gheo5l.html.

16. Chick Corea, *The Meeting*, with Friedrich Gulda, © 1983 by Philips 410 397-1, compact disc.

17. Obituary for Friedrich Gulda, *Guardian*, January 31, 2001, http://www.theguardian.com/news/2000/feb/01/guardianobituaries.

18. Panken, interview with Chick Corea, 23.

19. Tim Page, "Music: Chick Corea Is Thinking a Lot about Mozart Now," *New York Times*: January 2, 1983.

20. William Stephenson, "Play (An Improvisation in Five Acts)," *Jazziz* 9, no. 25 (March/April 1992): 39.

21. Chick Corea, *Play*, with Bobby McFerrin, © 1992, 1992 by Blue Note Records CDP 7 95477 2, compact disc.

22. Chick Corea, *The Mozart Sessions*, with Bobby McFerrin, Saint Paul Chamber Orchestra, © 1996, 2014 by Sony Classical, Sony Classical 88843047122-23, compact disc.

23. Joseph Kerman, "Piano Concertos by Mozart and Beethoven," *Early Music* 25, no. 3 (August 1997): 519–21.

24. Chick Corea, *Duet*, with Hiromi, © 2007, 2008 by Stretch Records SCD-088072308275, compact disc.

25. Hiromi, *Another Mind*, with Dave DiCenso, Anthony Jackson, Dave Fiuczynski, Jim Odgren, © 2003, 2003 by Telarc CD-83558, compact disc.

26. Larry Appelbaum, "In Conversation with Hiromi," Jazz.com, 2009, http://www.jazz.com/features-and-interviews/2009/8/9/in-conversation-with-hiromi.

27. Chick Corea, *Rendezvous in New York*, © 2003, 2003 by Stretch Records SCD2-9041-2, compact disc.

28. William Ruhlmann, review of *Orvieto*, Allmusic.com, n.d., http://www.allmusic.com/album/orvieto-mw0002193286.

29. Sujin Thomas, Music Reporter. 2007. "Potent combination; Grammy-winning duo Gary Burton and Chick Corea will get their groove on at Mosaic." *Straits Times* (Singapore), March 15. NewsBank, EBSCOhost (accessed July 25, 2017).

30. Bela Fleck, *Tales from the Acoustic Planet*, © 1995, 1995 Warner Brothers CDW 45854, compact disc.

31. Chick Corea, *The Enchantment*, with Béla Fleck, © 2007, 2007 by Concord Records 7230253, compact disc.

32. Bill Meredith, "Rules Don't Apply," *JazzTimes* 37, no. 6 (August 2007): 61.

33. "Chick Corea and Bela Fleck on the Joys (and Challenges) of Collaborating," heard on NPR *All Things Considered*, September 19, 2015, http://www.npr.org/2015/09/19/441257596/chick-corea-and-b-la-fleck-on-the-joys-and-challenges-of-collaborating.

34. Thomas Conrad, "The New Crystal Silence," *JazzTimes*, May 2008,http://jazztimes.com/articles/18122-the-new-crystal-silence-chick-corea-amp-gary-burton.

7. ACOUSTIC VARIATIONS

1. Richard Guilliatt, "The Young Lions' Roar: Wynton Marsalis and the 'Neoclassical' Lincoln Center Orchestra Are Helping Fuel the Noisiest Debate since Miles Went Electric." *Los Angeles Times*, September 13, 1992, 6.

2. Ibid.

3. Chuck Berg, "Marsalis Revives Acoustic Jazz," *Salem Press Encyclopedia* Research Starters, January 2015, accessed August 3, 2016.

4. Chick Corea, *Three Quartets*, with Michael Brecker, Steve Gadd, Eddie Gomez, © 1981, 1981 by Warner Bros. Records BSK 3552, vinyl.

5. David Adler, "I Love It All," *JazzTimes* 42, no. 3 (April 2012).

6. Chris Collins, "Chick Corea: Communicating Change," *Jazz Educators Journal* 29, no. 3 (1996): 31.

7. Chick Corea, *Three Quartets*, © 1981 by Stretch Records STD-1103, compact disc.

8. Chick Corea, *Rendezvous in New York*, © 2003 by Stretch Records 038 023-2, compact disc.

9. "Chick Corea A Very Special Concert 1982 Full Concert," YouTube video, 56:38, posted by Oscar D'Arcangeli, May 12, 2012, https://www.youtube.com/watch?v=pUFmnZqEvP8.

10. Chick Corea, *Echoes of an Era*, with Chaka Khan, Freddie Hubbard, Joe Henderson, Stanley Clarke, Lenny White, © 1982, 1982 by Elektra E1-60021, vinyl.

11. Chick Corea, *Echoes of an Era 2 (The Concert)*, with Nancy Wilson, Joe Henderson, Stanley Clarke, Lenny White, © 1982, 1982 by Elektra 60165-1, vinyl.

12. As told in an interview with Lenny White by the author, August 29, 2016.

13. *The Griffith Park Collection*, Elektra E1-60025, LP: 1982.

14. Quoted in Carl Hager, "Hubbard/Henderson/Corea/Clarke/White: Echoes of a Hard Bop Era," AllAboutJazz.com, June 2, 2009, https://www.allaboutjazz.com/hubbard-henderson-corea-clarke-white-echoes-of-a-hard-bop-era-by-carl-l-hager.php.

15. Chick Corea, *Lyric Suite for Sextet*, with Gary Burton, © 1984 by ECM Records ECM 1260, vinyl.

16. Chick Corea, *Trio Music*, with Miroslav Vitous, Roy Haynes, © 1982, 1982 by ECM Records ECM 1232/33, 2 x vinyl.

17. Chick Corea, *Touchstone*, with Various Groups, © 1982, 1982 by Warner Bros. Records WB 57 015, vinyl.

18. Chick Corea, *Again and Again (The Joburg Sessions)*, © 1983, 1983 by Elektra Musician 60167, vinyl.

19. Chick Corea, *The Meeting*, with Friedrich Gulda, © 1983 by Philips 410 397-1, vinyl.

20. Collins, "Chick Corea," 33.

21. Chick Corea, *Trio Music*, with Miroslav Vitous, Roy Haynes, © 1982, 1982 by ECM Records ECM 1232/33, 2 x vinyl.

22. Ted Panken, Smithsonian Jazz Oral History Program NEA Jazz Masters Interview with Armando Anthony "Chick" Corea, p. 25, November 5, 2012, Archives Center, National Music of American History, Washington, DC.

23. Chick Corea, *Voyage*, with Steve Kujala, © 1985, 1985 by ECM Records, ECM Records ECM 1282, 823 468-2, compact disc.

24. Chick Corea, *Septet*, © 1985, 1985 by ECM Records, ECM Records 25035-1 E, ECM 1297, compact disc.

25. Chick Corea, *Trio Music, Live in Europe*, with Miroslav Vitous, Roy Haynes, © 1986, 1986 by ECM Records, ECM Records ECM 1310, B0011618-02, compact disc.

26. Chick Corea, *Children's Songs*, © 1984, 1984 by ECM Records ECM 1267, compact disc.

27. Don Heckman, "Chick Corea & the Akoustic Band," *JazzTimes* 21, no. 1 (February 1991): 28.

28. Lee Jeske, "Chick Corea," *DownBeat* 48, no. 6 (June 1981): 16–19.

8. BACK TO ELECTRIC

1. “NED History,” Synclavier, n.d., http://www.500sound.com/snedhistory.html.

2. Larry Mueth, “MIDI Technology for the Scared to Death,” *Music Educators Journal*, 1993, 49.

3. Patrick Cole, “Elektric Band: An Alignment of Positive Charges,” *Jazziz* 7, no. 5 (August/September 1990): 40.

4. Ted Panken, Smithsonian Jazz Oral History Program NEA Jazz Masters Interview with Armando Anthony “Chick” Corea, November 5, 2012, Archives Center, National Music of American History, Washington, DC.

5. Interview with John Patitucci by the author April 2, 2015.

6. Mitchell Feldman and Manni Van Bohr, “Chick Corea: Return to Return to Forever,” *Fachblatt Musik Magazin*, July 1986, 39.

7. Chick Corea Elektric Band, *The Chick Corea Elektric Band*, © 1986, 1986 by GRP, GRP-A-1026, LP.

8. Interview with John Patitucci by the author April 2, 2015.

9. Chick Corea Elektric Band, *Light Years*, © 1987, 1987 by GRP, GRD-9546, compact disc.

10. Interview with Jamie Glaser by the author August 15, 2015.

11. Cole, “Elektric Band,” 41.

12. Kirk Silsbee, “Chick-ology,” *DownBeat* 72, no. 2 (February 2005): 41.

13. Josef Woodard, “Piano Dreams Come True,” *DownBeat* 55, no. 9 (September 1988): 18.

14. Chick Corea Elektric Band, *Eye of the Beholder*, © 1988, 1988 by GRP, GRD-9564, compact disc.

15. Woodard, “Piano Dreams Come True,” 18.

16. Ibid.

17. Chick Corea Akoustic Band, *Chick Corea Akoustic Band*, © 1989, 1989 by GRP, GRD 9582, compact disc.

18. Panken, interview with Chick Corea, 22.

19. Daniel Gioffre, review of *Chick Corea Akoustic Band*, AllMusic.com, n.d., http://www.allmusic.com/album/chick-corea-akoustic-band-mw0000199498.

20. Fred Bouchard, “Chick Corea: Akoustic,” *DownBeat* 58, no. 2 (February 1991): 17.

21. Chick Corea Akoustic Band, *Alive*, © 1991, 1991 by GRP, GRD 9627, compact disc.

22. Bouchard, “Chick Corea,” 19.

23. Don Heckman, “Chick Corea & the Akoustic Band,” *JazzTimes* 21, no. 1 (February 1991): 32.

24. Chick Corea Elektric Band, *Inside Out*, © 1990, 1990 by GRP, GRD-9601, compact disc.

25. Chick Corea Elektric Band, *Beneath the Mask*, © 1991, 1991 by GRP, GRD-9649, compact disc.

26. Chick Corea Elektric Band, *To the Stars*, © 2003, 2003 by Stretch UCCJ-3013, compact disc.

27. Interview with John Patitucci by the author April 2, 2015.

28. Panken, interview with Chick Corea, 27.

29. John Patitucci, *Heart of the Bass*, © 1992, 1992 by Stretch SCD-9001-2, compact disc.

30. Zan Stewart, "Brave New Band," *DownBeat* 60, no. 12 (December 1993): 30–31.

31. Birnbaum, Larry. Paint the World. Chick Corea's Elektric Band II. *DownBeat* 10, no. 60 (October 1993): 34.

32. Chick Corea Elektric Band, *To the Stars*, © 2004, 2004 by Stretch UCCJ-3013, compact disc.

33. Kirk Silsbee, "Chick-ology," *DownBeat* 72, no. 2 (February 2005): 38.

34. L. Ron Hubbard, *To the Stars* (Hollywood, CA: Galaxy, 2004).

35. Chick Corea Quartet, *Time Warp*, © 1995, 1995 by Stretch STD-1115, compact disc.

36. Chick Corea, *The Mozart Sessions*, with Bobby McFerrin, Saint Paul Chamber Orchestra, © 1996, 2014 by Sony Classical, Sony Classical 88843047122-23, compact disc.

37. Chick Corea & Gary Burton, *Native Sense*, © 1997, 1997 by Stretch SCD-9014-2, compact disc.

38. Chick Corea, *Remembering Bud Powell*, with Friends, © 1997, 1997 by Stretch Records SLP-9012-1, compact disc.

39. Chick Corea, *"Spain" for Sextet & Orchestra / Piano Concerto No. 1*, with London Philharmonic Orchestra, © 1999, 1999 by Sony Classical, Stretch Records SK 61799, compact disc.

40. Judith Schlesinger, review of *"Spain" for Sextet & Orchestra / Piano Concerto No. 1*, AllMusic.com, n.d., http://www.allmusic.com/album/spain-piano-concerto-no-1-mw0000395674.

41. Interview with John Patitucci by the author April 2, 2015.

42. Ibid.

9. SO MANY THINGS TO DO

1. Alex Suskind, "15 Years after Napster: How the Music Service Changed the Industry," *Daily Beast*, June 6, 2014, retrieved September 7, 2016, http://

www.thedailybeast.com/articles/2014/06/06/15-years-after-napster-how-the-music-service-changed-the-industry.html.

2. Chick Corea New Trio, *Past, Present & Futures*, with Jeff Ballard, Avishai Cohen, © 2001, 2001 by Stretch SCD-9035-2, compact disc.

3. Paula Edelstein, review of *Past, Present & Futures*, AllMusic.com, n.d., retrieved October 17, 2016, at http://www.allmusic.com/album/past-present-futures-mw0000003106

4. Chick Corea, *Rendezvous in New York*, © 2003, 2003 by Stretch Records SCD2-9041-2, compact disc.

5. P. 11 in the liner notes for *Rendezvous in New York.*

6. Chick Corea Elektric Band, *To the Stars*, © 2004, 2004 by Stretch Records UCCJ-3013, compact disc.

7. Chick Corea and Trondheim Jazz Orchestra, *Live in Molde*, © 2005, 2005 by MNJ Records MNJ CD 001, compact disc.

8. Chick Corea and Touchstone, *Rhumba Flamenco*, with Carles Benavent, Tom Brechtlein, Rubem Dantas, Jorge Pardo, Gayle Moran Corea, © 2005, 2005 by Chick Corea Productions CCP-01, compact disc.

9. Chick Corea, *The Ultimate Adventure*, © 2006, 2006 by Stretch Records SCD-9045-2, compact disc.

10. John Kelman, review of *The Ultimate Adventure*, AllAboutJazz.com, February 4, 2006, retrieved on October 17, 2016, https://www.allaboutjazz.com/the-ultimate-adventure-chick-corea-stretch-records-review-by-john-kelman.php.

11. Chick Corea, Steve Gadd, Christian McBride, *Super Trio—Live at the One World Theatre, April 3, 2005*, © 2006, 2006 by Mad Hatter Productions MHP02, compact disc.

12. Chick Corea, *The Enchantment*, with Bela Fleck, © 2007, 2007 by Concord Records CCD-30253, compact disc.

13. Chick Corea, *Five Trios.* © 2007, 2007 by Stretch Records UCCJ-9089/94, compact disc.

14. Chick Corea, *The New Crystal Silence*, with Gary Burton, © 2008, 2008 by Concord Records CCD2-30630, compact disc.

15. Chick Corea, *Duet*, with Hiromi, © 2007, 2008 by Stretch Records SCD-088072308275, compact disc.

16. Return to Forever, *Returns*, © 2008, 2008 by Eagle Rock Entertainment ER 20149-2, compact disc.

17. Chick Corea, *Five Peace Band Live*, with John McLaughlin, © 2009, 2009 by Concord Records CRE-31397-02, compact disc.

18. Stuart Nicholson, "Peace Breaks Out," *Jazzwise*, no. 131 (January 2009): 28.

19. Chick Corea, *Forever*, with Stanley Clarke, Lenny White, © 2011, 2011 by Concord Records CRE-32627-2, compact disc.

20. Chick Corea, *Orvieto*, with Stefano Bollani, © 2011, 2011 by ECM Records, ECM Records 277 9692, compact disc.

21. Chick Corea, *Further Explorations*, with Eddie Gomez, Paul Motian, © 2012, 2012 by Concord Jazz CJA-33364-02, compact disc.

22. David Adler, "I Love It All," *JazzTimes* 42, no. 3 (April 2012): 41.

23. Chick Corea, *The Continents, Concerto for Jazz Quintet & Chamber Orchestra*, © 2012, 2012 by Deutsche Grammophon, Universal Music Group International 4605026710337, compact disc.

24. Return to Forever, *The Mothership Returns,* © 2012, 2012 by Eagle Rock Entertainment ER 20257-2, compact disc and DVD.

25. Chick Corea, *Hot House*, with Gary Burton, Harlem String Quartet, © 2012, 2012 by Concord Records CIA-33363-02, compact disc.

26. Chick Corea, *The Vigil*, with Charles Altura, Gayle Moran Corea, Hadrien Feraud, Marcus Gilmore, Pernell Saturnino, Ravi Coltrane, Stanley Clarke, Tim Garland, © 2013, 2013 by Concord Jazz CJA-34762-01, compact disc.

27. As noted on the back of the CD cover.

28. Chick Corea, *Solo Piano—Portraits*, © 2014, 2014 by ECM Records, Concord Records CIA-35603-02, compact disc.

29. Chick Corea, *Trilogy*, with Christian McBride, Brian Blade, © 2014, 2014 by Concord Records CIA-35685-02, compact disc.

30. Chick Corea, *Two*, with Bela Fleck, © 2015, 2015 by Concord Records CIA-37992-02, compact disc.

31. Marius Nordal, "Chick Corea: Further Explorations of Bill Evans," *DownBeat* 77, no. 6 (June 2010): 28.

CODA

1. Allen Morrison, "The Music Defies Words," *DownBeat* 81, no. 12 (December 2014): 38.

2. Ibid.

3. Chris Collins, "Chick Corea: Communicating Change," *Jazz Educators Journal* 29, no. 3 (1996): 28.

4. Ibid.

5. Mike Haid, "A Conversation with Chick Corea," *Music Connection* 21, no. 10 (1997): 33.

SELECTED DISCOGRAPHY

Corea, Chick. *The Musician*. With various ensembles. © 2016, 2016 by Concord Records CIA-00019.3 3 x compact disc and Blu-Ray.

Corea, Chick. *Two*. With Bela Fleck. © 2015, 2015 by Concord Records CIA-37992-02. Compact disc.

Corea, Chick. *Trilogy*. With Christian McBride, Brian Blade. © 2014, 2014 by Concord Records CIA-35685-02. Compact disc.

Corea, Chick. *Chick Corea Solo Piano—Portraits.* © 2014, 2014 by Concord Jazz. Concord Jazz—0888072356030. 2 x compact disc.

Corea, Chick. *The Vigil.* With Charles Altura, Gayle Moran Corea, Hadrien Feraud, Marcus Gilmore, Pernell Saturnino, Ravi Coltrane, Stanley Clarke, Tim Garland. © 2013, 2013 by Concord Jazz CJA-34762-01. Compact disc.

Corea, Chick. *Further Explorations.* With Eddie Gomez, Paul Motian. © 2012, 2012 by Concord Jazz CJA-33364-02. Compact disc.

Corea, Chick. *Hot House.* With Gary Burton, Harlem String Quartet. © 2012, 2012 by Concord Records CIA-33363-02. Compact disc.

Corea, Chick. *The Continents, Concerto for Jazz Quintet & Chamber Orchestra.* © 2012, 2012 by Deutsche Grammophon, Universal Music Group International 4605026710337. Compact disc.

Corea, Chick. *Return to Forever: The Mothership Returns.* With Return to Forever. © 2012, 2012 by Eagle Rock Entertainment ER 20257-2. Compact disc and DVD.

Corea, Chick. *Forever.* With Stanley Clarke & Lenny White. © 2011, 2011 by Concord Records CRE-32627-2. 2 x compact disc.

Corea, Chick. *Orvieto.* With Stefano Bollani. © 2011, 2011 by ECM Records ECM 2222. Compact disc.

Corea, Chick. *Five Peace Band Live.* With John McLaughlin, Vinnie Colaiuta, Kenny Garrett, Christian McBride. © 2009, 2009 by Concord Records Concord 8880072313972. 2 x compact disc.

Corea, Chick. *Electric Chick: Compilation.* © 2008, 2008 Verve Records 06007 5306462. Compact disc.

Corea, Chick. *The New Crystal Silence.* With Gary Burton. © 2008, 2008 by Concord Records CCD2-30630. Compact disc.

Corea, Chick. *Return to Forever: Returns.* With Return to Forever. © 2008, 2008 by Eagle Rock Entertainment ER 20149-2. Compact disc.

Corea, Chick. *Duet.* With Hiromi. © 2007, 2008 by Stretch Records SCD-088072308275. Compact disc.

Corea, Chick. *Five Trios.* © 2007, 2007 by Stretch Records UCCJ-9089/94. Compact disc.

Corea, Chick. *The Enchantment.* With Béla Fleck. © 2007, 2007 by Concord Records CCD-30253. Compact disc.

Corea, Chick. *The Mystery.* With Northern Sinfonia, Tim Garland. © 2007, 2007 by Audio-B ABCD 5020. Compact disc.

Corea, Chick. *The Ultimate Adventure.* With Tom Brechtlein, Vinnie Colaiuta, Frank Gambale, Tim Garland, Hubert Laws. © 2006, 2006 by Stretch Records SCD-9045-2. Compact disc.

Corea, Chick, Steve Gadd, Christian McBride. *Super Trio—Live at the One World Theatre, April 3rd, 2005.* © 2006, 2006 by Mad Hatter Productions MHP02. Compact disc.

Corea, Chick. *Live in Molde.* With Trondheim Jazz Orchestra. © 2005, 2005 by MNJ Records MNJ CD 001. Compact disc.

Corea, Chick, and Touchstone. *Rhumba Flamenco.* With Carles Benavent, Tom Brechtlein, Rubem Dantas, Jorge Pardo, Gayle Moran Corea. © 2005, 2005 by Chick Corea Productions CCP-01. Compact disc.

Chick Corea Elektric Band. *To the Stars.* With Frank Gambale, Eric Marienthal, John Patitucci, Dave Weckl. © 2004, 2004 by Stretch UCCJ-3013. Compact disc.

Corea, Chick. *Rendezvous in New York.* Various ensembles. © 2003, 2003 by Stretch Records SCD2-9041-2. Compact disc.

Corea, Chick. *Marian McPartland's Piano Jazz.* © 2002, 2002 by the Jazz Alliance TJA-12040-2. Compact disc.

Corea, Chick. *A Very Special Concert.* With Stanley Clarke, Joe Henderson, Lenny White. © 2002, 2003 by Image Entertainment Inc. ID3226NBDVD. Compact disc.

Corea, Chick. *Keyboard Workshop—Methods of Composition, Improvisation and Practice.* © 2002, 2002 by Warner Bros. Music 904912. DVD.

Chick Corea New Trio. *Past, Present & Futures.* With Jeff Ballard, Avishai Cohen. © 2001, 2001 by Stretch SCD-9035-2. Compact disc.

Corea, Chick. *Solo Piano: Originals (Part One).* © 2000, 2000 by Stretch Records SCD-9029-2. Compact disc.

Corea, Chick. *Solo Piano: Standards (Part Two).* © 2000, 2000 by Stretch Records SCD-9028-2. Compact disc.

Corea, Chick. *Seabreeze.* © 2000, 2000 by Past Perfect Silver Line 204233-203. Compact disc.

Corea, Chick. *"Spain" for Sextet & Orchestra / Piano Concerto No. 1.* With London Philharmonic Orchestra. © 1999, 1999 by Sony Classical, Stretch Records SK 61799. Compact disc.

Corea, Chick. *Converge.* With Dave Holland, Jack DeJohnette, Hubert Laws, Bennie Maupin, Woodie Shaw. © 1999, 1999 by West Wind WW 2116. Compact disc.

Corea, Chick. *Change.* With Origin. © 1999, 1999 by Stretch Records SCD-9023-2. Compact disc.

Corea, Chick. *Live at the Blue Note.* With Origin. © 1998, 1998 by Stretch Records SCD-9018-2. Compact disc.

Corea, Chick. *Like Minds.* With Gary Burton, Roy Haynes, Dave Holland, Pat Metheny. © 1998, 1998 by Concord Records, Concord Jazz CCD-4803-2. Compact disc.

Corea, Chick. *A Week at the Blue Note.* With Origin. © 1998, 1998 by Stretch Records SCD6-9020-2. 6 x compact disc.

Corea, Chick. *Native Sense.* With Gary Burton. © 1997, 1997 by Stretch SCD-9014-2. Compact disc.

Corea, Chick. *Woodstock Jazz Festival.* With Anthony Braxton, Jack DeJohnette, Lee Konitz, Pat Metheny, Miroslav Vitous. © 1997, 1998 by Gravity Limited, Pioneer Artists PA-11672. Compact disc.

Corea, Chick. *Remembering Bud Powell.* With Kenny Garrett, Roy Haynes, Christian McBride, Joshua Redman, Wallace Roney. © 1997, 1997 by Stretch Records SCD-9012-2. Compact disc.

Corea, Chick. *4tune.* With John Dentz, Andrew Simpkins, Ernie Watts. © 1997, 1997 by West Wind WW 2105. Compact disc.

Corea, Chick. *The Gold Collection.* With Dave Holland, Jack DeJohnette, Hubert Laws, Woody Shaw. © 1997, 1969 by Recording Arts SA R2CD 40-28. 2 x compact disc.
Chick Corea Elektric Band. *Live from Elario's.* With John Patitucci, Dave Weckl. © 1996, 1996 by Stretch MVCR-239. Compact disc.
Corea, Chick. *The Mozart Sessions.* With Bobby McFerrin, Saint Paul Chamber Orchestra. © 1996, 1996 by Sony Classical, Sony Classical SK 62601. Compact disc.
Corea, Chick. *Return to the 7th Galaxy: The Anthology.* With Return to Forever. © 1996, 1996 by Verve Records 533 108-2. 2 x compact disc.
Corea, Chick. *Music Forever & Beyond: The Selected Works of Chick Corea 1964–1996.* © 1996, 1996 by GRP, GRD-5-9819. 5 x compact disc.
Corea, Chick. *The Trio Live from Country Club.* With Roy Haynes, Miroslav Vitous. © 1982, 1996 by Stretch Records MVCR-243. Compact disc.
Corea, Chick. *The Beginning.* © 1996, 1996 by LaserLight Digital, LaserLight Digital—17 083. Compact disc.
Chick Corea Quartet. *Time Warp.* With Bob Berg, Gary Novak, John Patitucci. © 1995, 1995 by Stretch STD-1115. Compact disc.
Corea, Chick. *Expressions.* © 1994, 1994 by GRP, GRD-9774. Compact disc.
Corea, Chick. *Live in Montreux.* With Joe Henderson, Roy Haynes, Gary Peacock. © 1994, 1994 by Stretch Records SCD-9009-2. Compact disc.
Chick Corea Elektric Band II. *Paint the World.* With Jimmy Earl, Eric Marienthal, Mike Miller, Gary Novak. © 1993, 1993 by GRP, GRD-9731. Compact disc.
Corea, Chick. *Play.* With Bobby McFerrin. © 1992, 1992 by Blue Note Records CDP 7 95477 2. Compact disc.
Chick Corea Elektric Band. *Beneath the Mask.* With Frank Gambale, Eric Marienthal, John Patitucci, Dave Weckl. © 1991, 1991 by GRP, GRD-9649. Compact disc.
Corea, Chick. *Variations on a Theme of Thelonius Monk.* © 1991, 1991 by Philips 23.10.002. Laserdisc.
Chick Corea Akoustic Band. *Alive.* With John Patitucci, Dave Weckl. © 1991, 1991 by GRP, GRD 9627. Compact disc.
Chick Corea Elektric Band. *Inside Out.* With Frank Gambale, Eric Marienthal, John Patitucci, Dave Weckl. © 1990, 1990 by GRP, GRD-9601. Compact disc.
Chick Corea Akoustic Band. *Chick Corea Akoustic Band.* With John Patitucci, Dave Weckl. © 1989, 1989 by GRP, GRD 9582. Compact disc.
Corea, Chick. *GRP Super Live in Concert.* With Dave Grusin, Lee Ritenour, Diane Schuur, Tom Scott. © 1988, 1988 by GRP, GR-2-1650. 2 x compact disc.
Chick Corea Elektric Band. *Eye of the Beholder.* With Frank Gambale, Eric Marienthal, John Patitucci, Dave Weckl. © 1988, 1988 by GRP, GRD-9564. Compact disc.
Corea, Chick. *Works for Piano by Mozart, Corea, and Gulda.* With Friedrich Gulda, Concertgebouw Orchestra, Nikolaus Harnoncourt. © 1987, 1987 by Musical Heritage Society MHS 827551K. Vinyl.
Corea, Chick Corea Elektric Band. Light years. With Frank Gambale, Eric Marienthal, John Patitucci, Dave Weckl,© 1987, 1987 by GRP, GRD-9546. Compact disc.
Corea, Chick. *Trio Music, Live in Europe.* With Miroslav Vitous, Roy Haynes. © 1986, 1986 by ECM Records, ECM Records ECM 1310, B0011618-02. Compact disc.
Corea, Chick. *Music for Three Guitars.* With de Falla Trio. © 1986, 1986 by Concord Concerto CCD-42011. Compact disc.
Chick Corea Elektric Band. *The Chick Corea Elektric Band.* With Scott Henderson, John Patitucci, Dave Weckl. © 1986, 1986 by GRP, GRP-A-1026. LP.
Corea, Chick. Hubert Laws, Quincy Jones. *Blanchard: New Earth Sonata Telemann: Suite in a Minor (Overture/Air A L'Italien/Rejouissance).* © 1985, 1985 by CBS Masterworks M 39858. Compact disc.
Corea, Chick. *Voyage.* With Steve Kujala. © 1985, 1985 by ECM Records ECM 1282. Compact disc.
Corea, Chick. *Septet.* © 1985, 1985 by ECM Records, ECM Records 25035-1 E, ECM 1297. Compact disc.

Gomez, Eddie. *Gomez.* With Chick Corea, Steve Gadd. © 1984, 1984 by Interface (3) 38C38-7189. Compact disc.
Corea, Chick. *Lyric Suite for Sextet.* With Gary Burton. © 1984 by ECM Records ECM 1260. Vinyl.
Honda, Toshiyuki. *Dream.* With Chick Corea, Roy Haynes, Miroslav Vitous. © 1984, 1984 by Eastworld EWJ-900027A-B. Compact disc.
Corea, Chick. *Children's Songs.* © 1984, 1984 by ECM Records ECM 1267. Compact disc.
Corea, Chick. *Double Concerto / Compositions.* With Friedrich Gulda, Concertgebouw Orchestra, Nikolaus Harnoncourt. © 1984, 1984 by TELDEC, TELDEC 6.42 961, 6.42961 AZ. Vinyl.
Friesen, David. *Amber Skies.* With Chick Corea, Joe Henderson, Paul Horn, Airto Moreira, Paul Motian. © 1983, 1983 by West Wind WW 2099. Compact disc.
Corea, Chick. *The Meeting.* With Friedrich Gulda. © 1983 by Philips, Philips Digital Classics 410 397-1. Vinyl.
Corea, Chick. *Fantasy for Two Pianos.* With Friedrich Gulda. © 1983, 1983 by TELDEC 6.20338. Vinyl.
Corea, Chick. *Again and Again (The Joburg Sessions).* With Don Alias, Carlos Benavent, Tom Brechtlein, Steve Kujala. © 1983, 1983 by Elektra Musician 60167. Vinyl.
Corea, Chick. *The Griffith Park Collection 2: In Concert.* With Stanley Clarke, Joe Henderson, Freddie Hubbard, Lenny White. © 1983, 1983 by Elektra Musician E1-60025. Vinyl.
Corea, Chick. *On Two Pianos.* With Nicolas Economou. © 1983, 1983 by Deutsche Grammophon 410 637-2. Compact disc.
Corea, Chick. *Echoes of an Era.* With Chaka Khan, Freddie Hubbard, Joe Henderson, Stanley Clarke, Lenny White. © 1982, 1982 by Elektra E1-60021. Vinyl.
Corea, Chick. *Echoes of an Era 2 (The Concert).* With Nancy Wilson, Joe Henderson, Stanley Clarke, Lenny White. © 1982, 1982 by Elektra 60165-1. Vinyl.
Corea, Chick. *Trio Music.* With Miroslav Vitous, Roy Haynes. © 1982, 1982 by ECM Records ECM 1232/33. 2 x vinyl.
Corea, Chick. *The Bennie Wallace Trio & Chick Corea.* With Bennie Wallace Trio. © 1982, 1982 by Enja Records 4028. Vinyl.
Corea, Chick. *Touchstone.* With various groups. © 1982, 1982 by Warner Bros Records WB 57 015. Vinyl.
Corea, Chick. *Three Quartets.* With Michael Brecker, Steve Gadd, Eddie Gomez. © 1981, 1981 by Warner Bros. Records BSK 3552. Vinyl.
Corea, Chick. *Europa Jazz.* With Dave Holland, Hubert Laws, Woody Shaw. © 1981, 1981 by Europa Jazz EJ-1003. Vinyl.
Burton, Gary. *Gary Burton.* With Chick Corea, Roy Haynes, Tiger Okoshi, Steve Swallow. © 1981, 1981 by Polydor, Polydor-115 2910. Vinyl.
Corea, Chick. *Chick & Lionel Live at Midem.* With Lionel Hampton. © 1980, 1980 by Who's Who in Jazz WW LP21016. Vinyl.
Corea, Chick. *The Griffith Park Collection.* With Stanley Clarke, Joe Henderson, Freddie Hubbard, Lenny White. © 1980, 1980 by Elektra Musician E1-60025. Compact disc.
Corea, Chick. *In Concert, Zürich, October 28, 1979.* With Gary Burton. © 1980, 1980 by ECM Records ECM-2-1182. 2 x vinyl.
Corea, Chick. *Tap Step.* With Bunny Brunel, Joe Farrell, Tom Brechtlein. © 1980, 1980 by Warner Bros. Records BSK 3425. Vinyl.
Corea, Chick. *Grandi Del Jazz.* With Return to Forever and Circle. © 1980, 1980 by Fabbri Editori. GdJ 86. Vinyl.
Henderson, Joe. *Mirror, Mirror.* With Ron Carter, Chick Corea, Billy Higgins. © 1980, 1980 by MPS Records MPS 15541. Vinyl.
Corea, Chick. *Waltz for Bill Evans.* With Horace Arnold, Dave Holland, Hubert Laws. © 1980, 1980 by Philips 16 PJ-2001. Vinyl.
Corea, Chick. *Delphi 2&3 Solo Piano Improvisations.* © 1980, 1980 by Polydor PD-2-6334. Vinyl.
Corea, Chick. *The Best of Return to Forever.* With Return to Forever. © 1980, 1980 by Columbia JC 36359. Vinyl.

Corea, Chick. *Jazzman.* © 1979, 1979 by 51 West Q 16078. Compact disc.
Corea, Chick. *Delphi 1 Solo Piano Improvisations.* © 1979, 1979 by Polydor PD-1-6208. Vinyl.
Corea, Chick. *Bouquet.* With Herbie Hancock. © 1979, 1979 by Polydor 424 551-1. Vinyl.
Corea, Chick. *Duet.* With Gary Burton. © 1979, 1979 by ECM Records ECM M5E 1140. Vinyl.
Corea, Chick. *Secret Agent.* With Joe Farrell, Bunny Brunel, Tom Brechtlein. © 1978, 1978 by Polydor PD-1-6176. Vinyl.
Corea, Chick. *The Sun.* © 1978, 1978 by Far East, Express ETJ-60004. Compact disc.
Corea, Chick. *Return to Forever—Live.* With Return to Forever. © 1978, 1978 by Columbia, Columbia C4X 35350. 4 x vinyl.
Corea, Chick. *Friends.* With Joe Farrell, Eddie Gomez, Steve Gadd. © 1978, 1978 by Polydor PD-1-6160. Vinyl.
Corea, Chick. *The Mad Hatter.* With Herbie Hancock, Eddie Gomez, Steve Gadd. © 1978, 1978 by the Mad Hatter PD-1-6130. Vinyl.
Corea, Chick. *Circulus.* With David Altschul, Anthony Braxton, Dave Holland. © 1978, 1978 by Blue Note BN-LA882-J2. 2 x vinyl.
Corea, Chick. *An Evening with Herbie Hancock & Chick Corea: In Concert.* With Herbie Hancock. © 1978, 1978 by Columbia PC2 35663. Vinyl.
Corea, Chick. *Circulus Vol. 1.* With Barry Altschul, Dave Holland. © 1978, 1978 by Blue Note 2S 062 61900. Vinyl.
Corea, Chick. *Musicmagic.* With Return to Forever. © 1977, 1977 by Columbia PC 34682, Vinyl.
Corea, Chick. *My Spanish Heart.* With Stanley Clarke, Steve Gadd, Don Alias. © 1976, 1976 by Polydor PD-2-9003. Compact disc.
Corea, Chick. *The Leprechaun.* With Joe Farrell, Anthony Jackson, Eddie Gomez, Steve Gadd. © 1976, 1976 by Polydor PD 6062. Vinyl.
Corea, Chick. *Romantic Warrior.* With Return to Forever. © 1976, 1976 by Columbia PC 34076. Vinyl.
Corea, Chick. *Chick Corea, Herbie Hancock, Keith Jarrett, McCoy Tyner.* With Herbie Hancock, Keith Jarrett, McCoy Tyner. © 1976, 1976 by Atlantic SD 1696. Compact disc.
Corea, Chick. *Chick Corea.* With Barry Altschul, Horace Arnold, Jack DeJohnette, Dave Holland, Hubert Laws, Benny Maupin, Woody Shaw, Miroslav Vitous. © 1975, 1975 by Blue Note BN-LA395-H2. Vinyl.
Corea, Chick. *No Mystery.* With Return to Forever. © 1975, 1975 by Polydor PD 6512. Vinyl.
Corea, Chick. *Circling In.* With Barry Altschul, Anthony Braxton, Dave Holland, Roy Haynes, Miroslav Vitous. © 1975, 1975 by Blue Note BN-LA472-H2. 2 x vinyl.
Joe Farrell Quartet. *Super Session.* With Chick Corea, John McLaughlin. © 1975, 1975 by CTI Records CTI 6003. Vinyl.
Corea, Chick. *Where Have I Known You Before.* With Return to Forever. © 1974, 1974 by Polydor PD 6509. Vinyl.
Corea, Chick. *Piano Giants.* With Mike Longo. © 1974, 1974 by Groove Merchant GM-4406. 2 x vinyl.
Corea, Chick. *Hymn of the Seventh Galaxy.* With Return to Forever. © 1973, 1973 by Polydor PD 5536. Vinyl.
Corea, Chick. *Light as a Feather.* With Return to Forever. © 1973, 1973 by Polydor 2310 247. Vinyl.
Clarke, Stan. *Children of Forever.* With Andy Bey, Dee Dee Bridgewater, Chick Corea, Lenny White, Pat Martino, Arthur Webb. © 1973, 1973 by Polydor PD 5531. Vinyl.
Corea, Chick. *Inner Space.* With Ron Carter, Joe Farrell, Hubert Laws, Steve Swallow, Grady Tate, Woody Shaw. © 1973, 1973 by Atlantic SD 2-305. Vinyl.
Corea, Chick. *Crystal Silence.* With Gary Burton. © 1973, 1973 by ECM Records ECM 1024 ST. Vinyl.
Corea, Chick. *Return to Forever.* With Return to Forever. © 1972, 1972 by ECM Records 78118 21022-4. Vinyl.

Corea, Chick. *Piano Improvisations, Vol. 2.* © 1972, 1972 by ECM Records, Polydor ECM 1020 ST. Compact disc.

Corea, Chick. *Sundance.* With Horace Arnold, Dave Holland, Jack DeJohnette, Hubert Laws, Woody Shaw. © 1972, 1972 by Groove Merchant GM 2202. Vinyl.

Corea, Chick. *A.R.C.* With David Holland, Barry Altschul. © 1971, 1971 by ECM Records, Polydor ECM-1-1009. Compact disc.

Corea, Chick. *Piano Improvisations, Vol. 1.* © 1971, 1971 by ECM Records, Polydor ECM 1014 ST, 2391 108. Compact disc.

Corea, Chick. *Going to the Rainbow.* With Rolf Kühn Jazz Group. © 1971, 1971 by BASF CRC 008. Vinyl.

Corea, Chick. *The Song of Singing.* With Barry Altschul, Dave Holland. © 1971, 1971 by Blue Note BST 84353. Vinyl.

Corea, Chick. *Circle 2: Gathering.* With Barry Altschul, Anthony Braxton, Dave Holland. © 1971 by CBS, CBS/ Sony—SOPL-20-XJ. Vinyl.

Corea, Chick. *Circle 1: Live in Germany Concert.* With Barry Altschul, Anthony Braxton, Dave Holland. © 1970, 1970 by CBS. CBS/Sony—SOPL-19-XJ. Vinyl.

Davis, Miles. *Bitches Brew.* With Chick Corea, Harvey Brooks, Don Alias, Jack DeJohnette, Lenny White, Dave Holland, John McLaughlin, Bennie Maupin, Joe Zawinul, Larry Young, Wayne Shorter. © 1970, 1970 by Columbia GP 26. 2 x vinyl.

Corea, Chick. *Is.* With Horace Arnold, Jack DeJohnette, Dave Holland, Hubert Laws, Woody Shaw. © 1969, 1969 by Solid State Records (2) SS 18055. Vinyl.

Davis, Miles. *In a Silent Way.* With Chick Corea, Herbie Hancock, John McLaughlin, Wayne Shorter, Dave Holland, Tony Williams. © 1969, 1969 by Columbia CS 9875. Vinyl.

Corea, Chick. *Tones for Joan's Bones.* With Joe Chambers, Joe Farrell, Steve Swallow, Woody Shaw. © 1968, 2004 by Vortex Records (2). Vinyl.

Corea, Chick. *Now He Sings, Now He Sobs.* With Roy Haynes, Miroslav Vitous. © 1968, 1968 by Solid State Records (2) SS18039. Vinyl.

Corea, Chick. *Village Vanguard Live Sessions 1.* With Pepper Adams, Richard Davis, Dizzy Gillespie, Elvin Jones, Mel Lewis, Ray Nance. © 1990, 1967 by Lester Recording Catalog CDC 9011. Compact disc.

Corea, Chick. *Village Vanguard Live Sessions 2.* With Pepper Adams, Garnett Brown, Richard Davis, Joe Farrell, Dizzy Gillespie, Elvin Jones, Marvin Stamm. © 1990, 1967 by Lester Recording Catalog CDC 9012. Compact disc.

Corea, Chick. *Live at Newport '67.* With Booker Ervin Quartet. © 1967, 2014 by Paradox Records Paradox Records (10)—630930. Compact disc.

La Roca, Pete. *Turkish Women at the Bath.* With Walter Booker, Chick Corea, John Gilmore. © 1967, 1967 by Douglas SD 782. Vinyl.

Mitchell, Blue. *The Thing to Do.* With Junior Cook, Chick Corea, Gene Taylor, Aloysius Foster. © 1965, 1965 by Blue Note BST 84178. Vinyl.

Stitt, Sonny. *Stitt Goes Latin.* With Willie Bobo, Chick Corea, Larry Gales, Thad Jones. © 1963, 1963 by Roost, Royal Roost SLP 2253. Vinyl.

SELECTED READING

Adler, David. "I Love It All." *JazzTimes* 42, no. 3 (April 2012): 38–41.
Andrew, Geoff. "Picturing New Sounds." *Aesthetica* no. 63 (2015): 134–37.
Bangs, Lester. "In a Silent Way." *Rolling Stone*, November 15, 1969.
Berg, Chuck. "Marsalis Revives Acoustic Jazz." *Salem Press Encyclopedia* Research Starters, January 2015. Accessed August 3, 2016.
Birnbaum, Larry. "Paint the World: Chick Corea's Elektric Band II." *DownBeat* 60, no. 10 (October 1993): 34.
Bogdanov, Vladimir, Chris Woodstra, and Stephen Thomas Erlewine. *All Music Guide: The Definitive Guide to Popular Music*. San Francisco: Backbeat Books/All Media Guide, 2001.
Bouchard, Fred. "Chick Corea: Akoustic." *DownBeat* 58, no. 2 (February 1991): 16–19.
Booth, Philip. "Sketching a Perfect Circle." *Jazziz* 15, no. 12 (December 1998): 44–48.
Cole, Patrick. "Elektric Band: An Alignment of Positive Charges." *Jazziz* 7, no. 5 (August/September 1990): 37–41, 54.
Collins, Chris. "Chick Corea: Communicating Change." *Jazz Educators Journal* 29, no. 3 (1996): 26–29, 31–34.
Conrad, Thomas. "The New Crystal Silence." *JazzTimes*, May 2008. http://jazztimes.com/articles/18122-the-new-crystal-silence-chick-corea-amp-gary-burton.
Corea, Chick. "The Function of an Artist, Part 2." *DownBeat* 40, no. 9 (1973): 15.
Corydon, Bent. *L. Ron Hubbard: Messiah or Madman*. Rev. ed. Fort Lee, NJ: Barricade Books, 1996.
Darter, Tom. "Chick Corea: Multi-keyboard Giant." *Contemporary Keyboard* 11, no. 1 (September/October 1975): 20–23.
Dobbins, Bill, transcriber. *Chick Corea Piano Improvisations.* Rottenburg, Germany: Advance Music, 1990.
Duke, Daniel Alan. "The Piano Improvisations of Chick Corea: An Analytical Study." 1996. RILM Abstracts of Music Literature, EBSCOhost. Accessed June 16, 2015.
Dwyer, Michael. "Chick Corea's '70s Jazz Group Return to Forever Is Back." *Sydney Morning Herald*, February 7, 2011.
Enright, Ed. "A Target of Religious Discrimination." *DownBeat* 63, no. 10 (October 1996): 6.
Ephland, John. "High Dive: Chick Corea and Bela Fleck Thrive on the Challenge of the Improvised Duo." *DownBeat* 74, no. 9 (September 2007): 44–47.
Feldman, Mitchell, and Manni Van Bohr. "Chick Corea: Return to Return to Forever." *Fachblatt Musik Magazin*, July 1986, 34–40.

Fine, Eric. "Corea-Burton Duo Highlights Overlapping Opposites." *DownBeat* 74, no. 5 (2007): 20.

———. "Electric Recharge." *DownBeat* 77, no. 7 (2010): 13.

Frink, Nathan. "An Analysis of the Compositional Practices of Ornette Coleman as Demonstrated in His Small Group Recordings during the 1970s." Unpublished master's thesis, University of Pittsburgh, 2011. Retrieved at http://d-scholarship.pitt.edu/11849/1/Frink_Thesis_ETD_%285%29.pdf.

Fuchs, Tom. "Chick Corea: Konzert eines jazzers." *Piano-News: Magazin für Klavier und Flügel*, no. 6: 14–19, 1999.

Gioia, Ted. *The History of Jazz.* New York: Oxford University Press, 1997.

Gitler, Ira. *Swing to Bop: An Oral History of the Transition in Jazz in the 1940s.* New York: Oxford University Press, 1985.

Guilliatt, Richard. "The Young Lions' Roar: Wynton Marsalis and the 'Neoclassical' Lincoln Center Orchestra Are Helping Fuel the Noisiest Debate since Miles Went Electric." *Los Angeles Times*, September 13, 1992, 6.

Guregian, Elaine. "Chick Corea / Friedrich Gulda: The Meeting." *DownBeat*, December 1983, 42–43.

Haid, Mike. "A Conversation with Chick Corea." *Music Connection* 21, no. 10 (1997): 28–33.

Hale, James. "Bill Connors: New Identity." *DownBeat* 72, no. 4 (2005): 34–35.

Heckman, Don. "Chick Corea & the Akoustic Band." *JazzTimes* 21, no. 1 (February 1991): 13–15, 28, 32.

Herzig, Monika. *David Baker: A Legacy in Music*. Bloomington: Indiana University Press, 2011.

Hoyt, Alex. "How Chick Corea Wrote 'Spain.'" *Atlantic*, November 25, 2011.

Hubbard, L. Ron. *Dianetics: The Modern Science of Mental Health, a Handbook of Dianetic Therapy*. New York: Hermitage House, 1950.

———. *To the Stars*. Hollywood, CA: Galaxy, 2004.

Isacoff, Stuart. *A Natural History of the Piano.* New York: Knopf, 2011.

Jenkins, Willard. "Fusion Warriors." *DownBeat* 73, no. 5 (May 2006): 46–50.

Jeske, Lee. "Chick Corea." *DownBeat* 48, no. 6 (June 1981): 16–19.

"John McLaughlin." *Guitar Player* 26, no. 1 (January 1992): 79.

Kerman, Joseph. "Piano Concertos by Mozart and Beethoven." *Early Music* 25, no. 3 (August 1997): 519–21.

Klostermann, Berthold. "Chick Corea Forever." *Fono Forum*, July 2011, 52–54.

Knight, Bill. "Grateful Dead (Music Group)." *Salem Press Encyclopedia* Research Starters, 2015. EBSCOhost. Accessed May 26, 2015.

Kolosky, Walter. *Power, Passion and Beauty: The Story of the Legendary Mahavishnu Orchestra; The Greatest Band That Ever Was*. Cary, NC: Abstract Logix Books, 2006.

Lake, Steve, and Paul Griffiths, eds. *Horizons Touched: The Music of ECM*. London: Granta Books, 2007.

Lester, James. *Too Marvelous for Words: The Life and Genius of Art Tatum.* New York: Oxford University Press, 1995.

Lyons, Len. *The Great Jazz Pianists*. New York: Da Capo, 1983.

Mattingly, Rick. "Chick Corea." *Modern Drummer*, March 1991, 60–63.

Meltzer, David, ed. *Writing Jazz.* San Francisco: Mercury House, 1999.

Meredith, Bill. "Rules Don't Apply." *JazzTimes* 37, no. 6 (August 2007): 58–63.

Morrison, Allen. "The Music Defies Words." *DownBeat* 81, no. 12 (December 2014): 38–41.

Mueth, Larry. "MIDI Technology for the Scared to Death." *Music Educators Journal*, 1993, 49.

Nemeyer, Eric. "Chick Corea." *Jazz Inside* 3, no. 7 (February 2002): 4, 6, 8–9, 11–12, 14, 58–59.

Nicholson, Stuart. "Peace Breaks Out." *Jazzwise*, no. 131 (January 2009): 26–28.

———. "To Infinity and Beyond." *Jazzwise*, no. 95 (March 2006): 36–39.

Nordal, Marius. "Chick Corea: Further Explorations of Bill Evans." *DownBeat* 77, no. 6 (June 2010): 26–31.

Ouellette, Dan. "*Bitches Brew*: The Making of the Most Revolutionary Jazz Album in History." *DownBeat* 66, no. 12 (1999): 32–34, 36–37.

Page, Tim. "Music: Chick Corea Is Thinking a Lot about Mozart Now." *New York Times*, January 2, 1983.

Panken, Ted. Smithsonian Jazz Oral History Program NEA Jazz Masters interview with Armando Anthony "Chick" Corea. Conducted November 5, 2012. Archives Center, National Music of American History, Washington, DC.

Pekar, Harvey. Review of *Tones for Joan's Bones*. *DownBeat* 35, no. 25 (1968): 23.

Pullman, Peter. *Wail: The Life of Bud Powell.* Peter Pullman, 2012.

Rideout, Ernie. "Where Have We Heard Them Before? Chick Corea and Return to Forever Reunite to Remind Us of Some of the Greatest Fusion Ever." *Keyboard*, July 2008: 24ff. Biography in Context. Accessed February 26, 2016.

Robson, Andy. "Blast from the Past." *Jazzwise*, no. 122 (August 2008): 24–27.

Rosenthal, T. (1998, 01). "Freedom and taste." *Piano & Keyboard*, 28–34.

Runcie, John. "Chick Corea: Portrait of the Artist as Communicator." *Jazz Journal* 29, no. 8 (August 1976): 26–28.

Silsbee, Kirk. "Chick-ology." *DownBeat* 72, no. 2 (February 2005): 36–38, 40–41.

Solothurnmann, Jurg. "Chick Corea: Feel the Joy of Life." *Jazz Forum*, no. 34 (1975): 49–52.

Stephenson, William. "Play (An Improvisation in Five Acts)." *Jazziz* 9, no. 25 (March/April 1992): 37–43, 57–59.

Stewart, Zan. "Brave New Band." *DownBeat* 60, no. 12 (December 1993): 30–31.

Tamarkin, Jeff. "Chick & Hiromi." *JazzTimes* 39, no. 3 (April 2009): 39.

Taylor, Greg. "Scientology in the German Courts." *Journal of Law and Religion* 19, no. 1 (2003–2004): 153–98.

Tingen, Paul. "The Making of *In a Silent Way* and *Bitches Brew*." Miles Beyond Articles retrieved at http://www.miles-beyond.com/iaswbitchesbrew.htm.

———. *Miles Beyond: The Electric Explorations of Miles Davis, 1967–1991*. New York: Billboard Books, 2001.

Toner, John. "Chick Corea." *DownBeat* 41, no. 6 (1974): 14–16.

Troupe, Quincy. "From Kind of Blue to Bitches Brew." In *Collected Work: Miles Davis and American Culture*, 118–29. St. Louis, MO: Missouri Historical Society Press, 2001. ISBN: 978-1-883982-37-9; 1-8839-8238-3. (AN: 2001-18020), n.p.: 2001. RILM Abstracts of Music Literature, EBSCOhost. Accessed March 2, 2015.

Underwood, Lee. "Armando in Wonderland." *DownBeat*, March 1978, 14–15.

———. "Chick Corea: Soldering the Elements, Determining the Future." *DownBeat* 43, no. 17 (October 1976): 13–14, 47–48.

Veal, Michael. "Miles Davis's Unfinished Electric Revolution." *Raritan* 22, no. 1 (2002): 153–63. Art Source, EBSCOhost, Accessed May 26, 2015.

Walser, Robert. *Keeping Time: Readings in Jazz History*. New York: Oxford University Press, 2014.

Woodard, Josef. "Chick Corea: The Next Chapter." *JazzTimes* 27, no. 2 (March 1997): 36–39.

———. "Kiss My Assets: Al Di Meola." *DownBeat* 59, no. 1 (January 1992): 21–23.

———. "Piano Dreams Come True." *DownBeat* 55, no. 9 (September 1988): 17–19.

Zagalaz, Juan. "The Jazz-Flamenco Connection: Chick Corea and Paco de Lucia between 1976 and 1982." *Journal of Jazz Studies* 8, no. 1 (Spring 2012): 33–54.

INDEX

Akoustic Band. *See* Chick Corea Akoustic Band
albums. *See* songs/works
Alias, Don, 3, 4
Altschul, Barry, 17, 24, 25, 28
A.R.C., 25, 28–29, 111n11
Armando and His Orchestra, 1
artistic philosophy, 51–52, 108; communication and, 27–28, 44, 106, 107; health and, 107–108; Hubbard, L. R., and, 36
Atschul, Barry, 28, 29
audiences, 43, 51. *See also* communication

Bach, Johann Sebastian, xiii
Bangs, Lester, 17
Barboza, Phil, 3
Bartok, Bela, 48–49
bebop, xviii–xx
Beneath the Mask, 82–83
Best of Return to Forever, 46
Bitches Brew, 13, 16, 19–20
Blade, Brian, 100, 106
Blake, Eubie, xv–xvi
Blood, Sweat & Tears, 20
Blue Note Jazz Club: in New York, 63, 92–93, 101; in Tokyo, 62–63, 96
blues, 10
Blues Incorporated, 14
Bollani, Stefano, 63, 98
boogie-woogie, xvii–xviii
bop. *See* bebop
brass bands, xiv, xv
Braxton, Anthony, 24–25
Brecker, Michael, 68–69, 73–75
Brown, Nacio Herb, 7
Burton, Gary: duets with, 57–59, 65–66, 96, 99; on *Lyric Suite for Sextet*, 69–70

cabaret tax, xviii
Captain Marvel, 34
career: in childhood, 2, 3; Circle and, 24–26; Davis and, 6, 13, 16–17, 24, 28; with Getz, 4–5, 33–34; in New York, early, 3–6; Stretch Records and, 83–84. *See also* Chick Corea Akoustic Band; Chick Corea Elektric Band; Return to Forever
"Carolina Shout", xvi, xvii
chamber jazz, 65, 68–69
Chick Corea Akoustic Band, 81–82, 84
Chick Corea and Touchstone, 94
Chick Corea and Trondheim Jazz Orchestra, 94
Chick Corea Elektric Band, 78; Chick Corea Akoustic Band and, 81–82; GRP Records and, 79–80; works by, 79–81, 82–83, 85, 93
Chick Corea Elektric Band II, 84–85
Chick Corea New Trio, 92
Chick Corea Solo Piano—Portraits, 100

Chick Corea Trio, 9–10
"Chick's Tune", 4, 6–9
childhood: career in, 2, 3; influences in, 1, 2, 3; piano in, 2
Children's Songs, 72, 100
Circle, 24–26, 28–29
Clarke, Kenny, xviii–xix, 97–98
Clarke, Stanley, 32; on Di Meola, 45; 1982 sessions with, 70–71; Return to Forever discussed by, 34–35, 43, 44, 46; on "Spain", 38, 39
classical music: improvisation in, xiv; jazz common space with, 72–73. *See also* chamber jazz; *Lyric Suite for Sextet*; neoclassic jazz; *Three Quartets*
Cobham, Billy, 14
Cohen, Avishai, 85–86
Coleman, Ornette, 23–24, 110n9
communication: artistic philosophy and, 27–28, 44, 106, 107; Return to Forever and, 42–43; Scientology and, 26, 31, 36; Silver and, 2–3
composition: of *Beneath the Mask*, 83; of "Got a Match", 87; of *The Mad Hatter*, 49; in Return to Forever, 44, 45
Concierto de Aranjuez, 38
Connors, Bill, 35, 43, 44, 45–46
The Continents, 98–99
contrafacts, 7
Cook, Junior, 6–9
Corea, Antonio, 1
Corea, Armando Anthony "Chick.". *See specific topics*
Corea, Armando John, 1
Corea.concerto, 86
Coryell, Larry, 14
Cristofori, Bartolomeo, xiii
Crystal Silence, 57–58, 65–66
"Crystal Silence", 65–66
Cuscuna, Michael, 27
cutting contests, xvi–xvii

Davis, Miles: *Bitches Brew* by, 13, 16, 19–20; Corea career and, 6, 13, 16–17, 24, 28; *Filles de Kilimanjaro* by, 15; *In a Silent Way* by, 13, 15–16, 17–19, 20; influence of, 9, 28, 38, 41–42; *Nefertiti* by, 28, 112n18; *Sketches of Spain* by, 38, 112n11; Third Great Quintet of, 24
Di Meola, Al, 44–46, 53
Dobbins, Bill, 27
drugs, 49, 80
drumming, 2, 4
"Duel of the Jester and the Tyrant", 52–54
duets: with Bollani, 63, 98; with Burton, 57–59, 65–66, 96, 99; with Fleck, 64, 95, 100–101; with Gulda, 60–61; with Hancock, 59–60; with Hiromi, 62–63, 96; with McFerrin, 61–62; with Rubalcaba, 63

Earl, Jimmy, 84
Echoes of an Era, 70
Echoes of an Era 2, 70
Editions of Contemporary Music (ECM), 25, 28, 29, 111n10–111n11
education, 2, 5, 106–107
Eicher, Manfred, 25, 28, 29, 36, 58, 65, 111n10
Elektric Band. *See* Chick Corea Elektric Band; Chick Corea Elektric Band II
Ellington, Duke, 81
Emergency, 14
The Enchantment, 64, 95
Evans, Bill, 98, 101–103
Evans, Gil, 38, 112n11
An Evening with Herbie Hancock and Chick Corea: In Concert, 59
Eye of the Beholder, 81

family, 1–2, 4
Farrell, Joe, 32–33, 38
Fender Rhodes, 6
"La Fiesta", 34, 65
Filles de Kilimanjaro, 15
Fitch, Bill, 3, 4
"500 Miles High", 34
Five Peace Band Live, 97
Five Trios, 95–96
flamenco, 94
Fleck, Bela, 64, 95, 100–101
Forever, 97–98
Foster, Al, 6–9
Four Sounds, 2
free jazz, 6, 24, 111n3
Free Jazz: A Collective Improvisation, 24, 110n9

Friends, 49–50
Further Explorations, 98, 101–103
fusion jazz, 13–14, 15, 41, 47

Gadd, Steve: *Hymn of the Seventh Galaxy* and, 41; on *Super Trio—Live at the One World Theatre*, 95; on *Three Quartets*, 68–69, 73–75
Gambale, Frank, 80; Chick Corea Elektric Band joined by, 80
Garland, Tim, 96
Germany, 26–27. *See also* Editions of Contemporary Music; Eicher, Manfred
Getz, Stan, 4–5, 33–34
Gillespie, Dizzy, xix, xx
Gilmore, John, 4
Gleason, Ralph, 16
Gomez, Eddie: *Further Explorations* with, 98, 101–103; on *Three Quartets*, 68–69, 73–75
Go Mongo, 3
"Got a Match", 86–89
Griffith Park Collections, 70, 71
Griffiths, Paul, 111n10
GRP Records: *The Chick Corea Elektric Band* and, 79–80; Stretch Records and, 83–84
Gulda, Friedrich, 60–61

Haden, Charlie, 23–24, 111n3
Haid, Mike, 51
Hall, Adelaide, xvii
Hammond, John, xviii
Hancock, Herbie, 3, 13, 59–60
"A Handful of Keys", xvii
Hart, Clyde, xx
Haynes, Roy, 6, 9–10, 71, 72
health, 107–108
Heart of the Bass, 83–84
Henderson, Joseph, 70–71
Henderson, Scott, 79, 80
Hendrix, Jimi, 15
Hill, Teddy, xviii
Hiromi Uehara, 62–63, 96
Holland, Dave: Davis, career and, 16–17, 24, 28; on "Nefertiti", 28, 29
Horizons Touched: The Music of ECM (Lake and Griffiths), 111n10
Hubbard, Freddie, 71
Hubbard, L. Ron, 26, 36, 85, 93, 94
Hymn of the Seventh Galaxy, 35, 41–42, 43

improvisation, xiv
In a Silent Way, 13, 15–16, 17–19, 20
influences: of Bartok, 48–49; in childhood, 1, 2, 3; of Davis, 9, 28, 38, 41–42; of Ellington, 81; of Getz, 5; of Gulda, 60–61; of Latin music, 3, 4; of Parker, 3; of Powell, xvi, xx; of Silver, 2–3; of Swallow, 4; of Wakeman, 52. *See also* Hubbard, L. Ron; Scientology
Inside Out, 82–83
"It's about That Time", 19

jam sessions, xviii–xx, 4
Japan, 34–35, 62–63, 96
jazz, xv; chamber form of, 65, 68–69; classical music common space with, 72–73; free form of, 6, 24, 111n3; neoclassic form of, 67–68; pianos, combos and, xviii; rock fusion with, 13–14, 15, 41, 47
Jazz Forum, 41–42
Jazz Masters Award, 105
Johnson, James P.: "Carolina Shout" by, xvi, xvii; cutting contests and, xvi, xvii
Joplin, Scott, xv
Jurek, Thom, 24; on *My Spanish Heart*, 48

Kahn, Gus, 7
Keeping Time: Readings in Jazz History (Walser), 111n3
Khan, Chaka, 70
Klarwein, Mati, 16
Korner, Alexis, 14
Kujala, Steve, 72

Lake, Steve, 111n10
La Roca, Pete, 4
Latin music: influence of, 3, 4; jam sessions and, 4; Moreira and, 33. *See also My Spanish Heart*
Led Zeppelin, 14
Lenox School of Jazz, 23
The Leprechaun, 46, 47

Lifetime, 14
Light as a Feather, 34–35, 37–39
Light Years, 80–81
"Litha", 4
Live at the Fillmore East March 7, 1970: It's about That Time, 24
Live in Molde, 94
Live in Paris, 25
London Philharmonic Orchestra, 86
Lundvall, Bruce, 70–71
Lyric Suite for Sextet, 69–70

Mabry, Betty, 15, 20
Macero, Teo, 15, 16, 18–19, 20
"Mademoiselle Mabry", 15
The Mad Hatter, 48–49
Mahavishnu Orchestra, 35, 42
Mann, Herbie, 5
Marienthal, Eric, 80
Marsalis, Wynton, 67
Massachusetts, 1–3
"Matrix", 9–10
Maupin, Bennie, 71
McBride, Christian: on *Super Trio—Live at the One World Theatre*, 95; *Trilogy* with, 100
McFerrin, Bobby, 61–62
McLaughlin, John, 14; *Five Peace Band Live* with, 97; on *In a Silent Way*, 15, 17–18; Mahavishnu Orchestra and, 35, 42; Return to Forever compared with, 42–43
The Meeting, 60–61
Metheny, Pat, 58
Mickman, Herbie, 5
MIDI. *See* Musical Instrument Digital Interface
Miles Beyond (Tingen), 110n8
Minton's Playhouse, xviii–xix, xx
Mitchell, Blue, 2, 4, 6–9
Mongo Santamaria band, 3
Monk, Thelonious, xviii–xix, xx, 72
Moran, Gayle, 46; Chick Corea Elektric Band and, 78–79; Mahavishnu Orchestra and, 42
Moreira, Airto: Return to Forever formation and, 33; on "Spain", 38
Morton, "Jelly Roll", xv
Moss, Ron, 80
Mothersbaugh, Jim, 77–78
The Mothership Returns, 99
Motian, Paul, 98, 101–103
Mozart, 60, 61
The Mozart Sessions, 62
Musical Instrument Digital Interface (MIDI), 77–78, 82, 86
Musician's Union, xix
Musicmagic, 46–47
Music Magic, 106
My Spanish Heart, 47–48

Napster, 91
National Endowment of the Arts (NEA), 105
Nefertiti, 28, 112n18
"Nefertiti", 25, 28–29
neoclassic jazz, 67–68
The New Crystal Silence, 58, 96
New York: Blue Note Jazz Club in, 63, 92–93, 101; cabaret tax in, xviii; career in, early, 3–6; family and, 4; jazz rock experiments in, 14
nickname, 2
1982: Clarke, S., sessions in, 70–71; collaborations in, various, 71; standards in, 71
1970s, 47, 51–52
1968, 13; *Filles de Kilimanjaro* sessions in, 15
No Mystery, 45
Novak, Gary, 84
Now He Sings, Now He Sobs, 6, 9–10

Origin, 86
Orvieto, 63, 98
Oxford Dictionary of Music Online, 112n5

Paint the World, 84–85
Parker, Charlie, xix, xx, 3, 33
Past, Present & Futures, 92
Patitucci, John: *Beneath the Mask* composition and, 83; in Chick Corea Akoustic Band, 81–82; Chick Corea Elektric Band and, 78–79, 80; on "Got a Match", 86–89; *Heart of the Bass* by, 83–84
Pekar, Harvey, 5–6

"Peri's Scope", 101–103
Perla, Gene, 4
piano, xiii–xiv; boogie-woogie technique for, xvii–xviii; in childhood, 2; Fender Rhodes electric, 6; ragtime and, xv; stride technique of, xvi–xvii
Piano Improvisations Volume 1, 27, 35–37
Piano Improvisations Volume 2, 27
Polydor, 37
Pomeroy, Herb, 2
Potter, Neville, 31
Powell, Bud, xvi, xx
Purim, Flora, 33, 38

"Quartet No. 1", 73–75

ragtime, xv
recording, xix, 15, 16, 18–19, 20, 64, 84
recording industry, 91–92
Red Hot Peppers, xv
Rendezvous in New York, 63, 92–93
rent parties, xvi–xvii
repertory orchestras, 67–68
Return to Forever, 112n5; audience of, 43; *Best of Return to Forever* by, 46; breakup of, 46; communication and, 42–43; composition in, 44, 45; Connors tenure in, 35, 43, 44; Di Meola joins, 44–46; "Duel of the Jester and the Tyrant" by, 52–54; *Forever* and, 97–98; formation of, 31–33; *Hymn of the Seventh Galaxy* by, 35, 41–42, 43; *Light as a Feather* by, 34–35, 37–39; McLaughlin compared with, 42–43; *The Mothership Returns* by, 99; *Musicmagic* by, 46–47; *Return to Forever* by, 34; *Return to Forever Returns* by, 50, 96; *Romantic Warrior* by, 45, 52–54; Scientology and, 31–32, 44
Rhumba Flamenco, 94
Ridley, Larry, 23
Roberts, Charles Luckeyeth "Luckey", xvi
rock, jazz fusion with, 13–14, 15, 41, 47
Rodrigo, Joaquin, 38, 112n11
Romantic Warrior, 45, 52–54
Rubalcaba, Gonzalo, 63

Santamaria, Mongo, 3
Schnabel, Artur, xiv
Schuller, Gunther, 73
Scientology, 26–27; communication and, 26, 31, 36; Return to Forever and, 31–32, 44. *See also* Hubbard, L. Ron
Secret Agent, 49, 50
Shorter, Wayne: on *Bitches Brew*, 20; on *In a Silent Way*, 17–18; "Nefertiti" by, 25, 28–29
sideslipping, 10
Silbermann, Gottfried, xiii
Silver, Horace, 2–3, 4, 6
Sissle, Noble, xvi
Sketches of Spain, 38, 112n11
Skomsvoll, Erlend, 94
Smith, Dave, 77–78
Smith, Willie "The Lion", xvi, xvii
solos: on "Bitches Brew", 20; on "Chick's Tune", 7–9; Getz influence on, 5; on "Got a Match", 87–89; on "Matrix", 10; on "Nefertiti", 28–29; on "Quartet No. 1", 74–75; on "Sometime Ago", 36–37
"Sometime Ago", 35–37
songs/works: *Bitches Brew*, 13, 16, 19–20; *Captain Marvel*, 34; *Change*, 86; *Chick Corea Akoustic Band*, 81–82; by Chick Corea Elektric Band, 79–81, 82–83, 85, 93; *Chick Corea Solo Piano—Portraits*, 100; "Chick's Tune", 4, 6–9; by Circle, 24–25, 28–29, 111n11; *The Continents*, 98–99; *Corea.concerto*, 86; *Echoes of an Era*, 70; *Echoes of an Era 2*, 70; "La Fiesta", 34, 65; *Filles de Kilimanjaro*, 15; *Five Trios*, 95–96; *Friends*, 49–50; *Further Explorations*, 98, 101–103; with Getz, 4; *Go Mongo*, 3; "Got a Match", 86–89; Griffith Park Collections, 70, 71; *In a Silent Way*, 13, 15–16, 17–19, 20; *The Leprechaun*, 46, 47; *Live at the Fillmore East March 7, 1970: It's about That Time*, 24; *Live in Molde*, 94; *Live in Paris*, 25; *Lyric Suite for Sextet*, 69–70; "Mademoiselle Mabry", 15; *The Mad Hatter*, 48–49; "Matrix", 9–10; *My Spanish Heart*, 47–48; "Nefertiti", 25, 28–29; *The New Crystal Silence*, 58, 96; *No Mystery*, 45; *Now He Sings, Now He Sobs*, 6, 9–10; *Paint the*

World, 84–85; *Past, Present & Futures*, 92; *Piano Improvisations Volume 1*, 27, 35–37; *Piano Improvisations Volume 2*, 27; "Quartet No. 1", 73–75; *Rendezvous in New York*, 63, 92–93; *Rhumba Flamenco*, 94; "Sometime Ago", 35–37; *Spaces*, 14; "Spain", 34, 37–39, 86; *Tales from the Acoustic Planet*, 64; *The Thing to Do*, 4, 6–9; *Three Quartets*, 68–69, 73–75; *Tones for Joan's Bones*, 5–6; *Trilogy*, 100; *Trio Music*, 71, 72; *Trio Music, Live in Europe*, 72; *Turkish Women at the Bath*, 4; *The Ultimate Adventure*, 94; various, 47, 71, 72; *The Vigil*, 100; *Where Have I Known You Before*, 45. *See also* duets; influences; Return to Forever

Spaces, 14
"Spain", 34, 37–39, 86
"Spinning Wheel", 20
standards, 71
Stretch Records, 83–84
stride piano, xvi–xvii
Sullo, Salvatore, 2
Super Trio—Live at the One World Theatre, 95
Swallow, Steve, 4
Sydney Symphony Orchestra, 96
Synclavier, 77, 78, 86
synthesizers, 54, 77, 78, 86, 87

Tales from the Acoustic Planet, 64
Tatum, Art, xvi–xvii
Taylor, Gene, 6–9
"Tea for Two", xvii
themes, 41–42
The Thing to Do, 4, 6–9
third-stream, 73
Three Quartets, 68–69, 73–75
"Tiger Rag", xvii
Time Warp, 85
Tingen, Paul, 110n8
Tokyo, 62–63, 96
Tones for Joan's Bones, 5–6
To The Stars, 85, 93
Trilogy, 100
Trio Music, 71, 72
Trio Music, Live in Europe, 72
Trondheim Jazz Orchestra, 94
Turkish Women at the Bath, 4
twenty-first century, 91
Two, 64, 100–101

The Ultimate Adventure, 94
Underwood, Lee, 48

Van Gelder Studio, 6–9
Vaughn, Sarah, 5
The Vigil, 100
Vitous, Miroslav, 6; "Matrix" with, 9–10; on *Spaces*, 14; on *Trio Music*, 71, 72
Vortex label, 5
Voyage, 72

Wakeman, Rick, 52
Waller, Maurice, xvii
Waller, Thomas "Fats", xvi, xvii
"Watermelon Man", 3
website, of Corea, 105–106
Weckl, Dave: *Beneath the Mask* composition and, 83; in Chick Corea Akoustic Band, 81–82; Chick Corea Elektric Band and, 78–79; on "Got a Match", 86–87, 88–89
Where Have I Known You Before, 45
White, Lenny, 41, 46, 52, 70, 97–98
whole tone scale, 8, 110n11
Williams, Mary Lou, xix
Williams, Tony, 6, 14
Wilson, Nancy, 70
"Windows", 4

Yamaha synthesizers, 78, 86, 87
Yellin, Pete, 3
Youmans, Vincent, xvii
"You Stepped Out of a Dream", 7–8

Zagalaz, Juan, 48
Zawinul, Joe, 17–18
Zombie music, xix

ABOUT THE AUTHOR

Monika Herzig holds a doctorate in music education with a focus on jazz studies from Indiana University where she is a senior lecturer in arts administration. She teaches courses on the music industry, programming, and arts entrepreneurship. Her research focus is on jazz as a model for creativity and entrepreneurship. She is also the author of *David Baker: A Legacy in Music*, published in 2011.

As a touring jazz artist, she has performed at many prestigious jazz clubs and festivals, such as the Indy Jazz Fest, New York's Birdland, Cleveland's Nighttown, and the W.C. Handy Festival, to name just a few. Groups under her leadership have toured Europe and Japan and opened for acts such as Tower of Power, Sting, the Dixie Dregs, Yes, and more.

She has released more than a dozen CDs under her leadership on her own ACME Records as well as Owl Studios and Whaling City Sounds. Her awards include a 1994 *DownBeat* magazine Award for Best Original Song, and a Jazz Journalist Association Hero 2015 Award, and she has been awarded grants from the NEA, the Indiana Arts Commission, and MEIEA (the Music and Entertainment Industry Educators Association), among others. Her recent project, "The Whole World in Her Hands," features the world's leading female jazz instrumentalists. Thomas Garner from Garageradio.com writes, "I was totally awed by the fine musicianship throughout."

More info and sound samples at www.monikaherzig.com.